Afro-Politics and Civ ____vador da Bahia, Brazil

UNIVERSITY PRESS OF FLORIDA

Florida A&M University, Tallahassee
Florida Atlantic University, Boca Raton
Florida Gulf Coast University, Ft. Myers
Florida International University, Miami
Florida State University, Tallahassee
New College of Florida, Sarasota
University of Central Florida, Orlando
University of Florida, Gainesville
University of North Florida, Jacksonville
University of South Florida, Tampa
University of West Florida, Pensacola

Afro-Politics and Civil Society
in Salvador da Bahia, Brazil

 Kwame Dixon

University Press of Florida

Gainesville · Tallahassee · Tampa · Boca Raton

Pensacola · Orlando · Miami · Jacksonville · Ft. Myers · Sarasota

Publication of this paperback edition made possible by a Sustaining the Humanities through the American Rescue Plan grant from the National Endowment for the Humanities.

First cloth printing, 2016
First paperback printing, 2022

27 26 25 24 23 22   6 5 4 3 2 1

Library of Congress Cataloging-in-Publication Data
Names: Dixon, Kwame, author.
Title: Afro-politics and civil society in Salvador da Bahia, Brazil / Kwame
    Dixon.
Description: Gainesville : University Press of Florida, [2016] | Includes
    bibliographical references and index.
Identifiers: LCCN 2015036779 | ISBN 9780813062617 (cloth) |
    ISBN 9780813068787 (pbk.)
Subjects: LCSH: Blacks—Brazil—Salvador—Politics and government. |
    Blacks—Brazil—Salvador—History. | Movimento Negro Unificado (Brazil) |
    Salvador (Brazil)—Race relations.
Classification: LCC F2519.1.B3 D59 2016 | DDC 305.800981/42—dc23
LC record available at http://lccn.loc.gov/2015036779

The University Press of Florida is the scholarly publishing agency for the State University System of Florida, comprising Florida A&M University, Florida Atlantic University, Florida Gulf Coast University, Florida International University, Florida State University, New College of Florida, University of Central Florida, University of Florida, University of North Florida, University of South Florida, and University of West Florida.

University Press of Florida
2046 NE Waldo Road
Suite 2100
Gainesville, FL 32609
http://upress.ufl.edu

This book is dedicated to my two daughters, Gabriela and Estrella, and their beloved grandmother Mae.

Contents

Figures

Acknowledgments

The idea to research and write a book on Salvador da Bahia stems from my long-standing interest in understanding the complexity of the Black presence in the Americas. While doing research in Cuba, Nicaragua, Ecuador, and Colombia in the mid- to late 1990s, I had always been fascinated, on one hand, and extremely intimidated, on the other, by Brazil: the vastness of the country, its language, its large and diverse Black population, its unique Afro–cultural formations, its sophisticated Black social movements. The scope, depth, and quality of the scholarship were, in my view, way too much for an Afro–North American from the southern part of the United States to negotiate. Simply put, I thought Brazil was way above and beyond my abilities. However, after making my first trip to Salvador in 1998 and returning ten years later in 2008, I decided that the time was ripe. After doing some preliminary research I was shocked to find that while there was a wealth of scholarship on Brazil, much of it ignored Salvador. I therefore came to the conclusion that this was a glaring omission as well as a "clear" blind spot in the literature. Since I had spent much of my time in Salvador and given my experience in the Black Americas, I decided to move forward with this ambitious project.

After finally convincing myself that I could do it, I soon came to the bold realization that this project would require other intricate moving parts to converge at different moments over time and space. Tom

Perrault, associate professor of geography and former director of the Program on Latin America and the Caribbean at Syracuse University, provided the first research grant to do some of the initial work in the summer of 2008. At the same time or shortly thereafter, Nancy Cantor (the chancellor of Syracuse University when most of the research was undertaken) also provided research monies for faculty in the humanities. These two initial sources of support paved the foundation for the first part of the research; later the College of Arts and Sciences at Syracuse University and George Langford (the former dean of the College of Arts and Sciences) as well as the Humanities Center provided research monies and time off to conduct field research and write. In the spring of 2012, I was a Humanities Center Faculty Fellow, which, along with research money, allowed for a two-course teaching release. It was time and money well needed. I am therefore deeply grateful to the College of Arts and Sciences.

In African American studies, Mĩcere Gĩthae Mũgo, renowned literary scholar and former chair of African American studies (Syracuse University), as well as her two beautiful daughters, Mũmbi wa Mũgo, and the younger daughter, Njeri Kũi Mũgo, provided deep inspiration and support. Njeri is no longer with us, but she did cutting-edge research on Brazil in the early 2000s. I also want to thank Rene Simson, who was chair of African American studies during the research and writing of this book. It goes without saying that having John Burdick, a leading scholar on Brazil, at Syracuse University was a dream come true and a luxury. He was generous, shared his time and knowledge, and always extended his support and solidarity. There were two outstanding undergraduate research assistants who were pivotal to this project: Ana Siberio and Ashlee Rossler. Ana Siberio, a double major in economics and international relations, worked toward the middle of the project researching articles and writing drafts; Ashlee Rossler, a double major in international relations and political science, worked at the very end of the project, ensuring all the materials were properly organized and keeping the project on track. They were both outstanding and I owe them a debt of gratitude.

In Salvador there are many to thank. Viviane de Jesus served as my research assistant, organizing visits, helping with the translations, and identifying key people and organizations as well as providing a critical lens to understand the complicated and fluid social landscape. She was central to the research and I owe her big time. And a very special thanks to Mario Nelson Carvalho; it was his interventions regarding the historical exclusion of Blacks from educational opportunities, which he linked to the lack of a robust Bahian Black intelligentsia, that helped me think more critically about the formation of Black social consciousness and political power or lack thereof in Brazil and Salvador. He was also gracious with his time, and he always invited me to his home for coffee and fresh fruit. It is important to mention the people at Steve Biko, Olodum, and Ilê Aiyê who allowed me access to their programs and students and shared their time generously. And a special thanks to members of the Salvador city council who shared their insights regarding local politics.

Harry Vanden, professor of political science, government, and international affairs at the University of South Florida, who was also my professor at USF, encouraged me, and I am grateful for his long-term support. A special thanks to Erika Stevens and the whole team at the University Press of Florida, who all worked hard to bring it all together. My family in Spain—Maria, Gabriela, and Estrella—deserve special mention as well as the whole Quesada family, who have all been extremely supportive throughout the project. Finally, my mother, Annie Mae Caldwell, who is no longer with us but remains a deep source of inspiration, would be proud.

Introduction

Brazil is the largest country in South America, the sixth-most populous country in the world with an estimated population of roughly 201.5 million (Instituto Brasileiro de Geografia e Estatítica / Brazilian Institute of Geography and Statistics 2014), and largely recognized as a thriving democracy with a federal system of government comprising twenty-six states and Brasília. It is now one of the BRICS countries (Brazil, Russia, India, China, and South Africa), which means that it has enormous potential, and within the next decade it is expected to become an economic and political juggernaut. In the last decade, the Brazilian economy significantly expanded its presence in world markets and global trade (Montero 2005, 117). Its national identity is largely defined by its complex and diverse multiethnic citizenry, its world famous carnival season, its soccer prowess, its rugged national politics, vibrant social movements, and sophisticated and well-organized civil society groups. In October of 2010, Brazil elected Dilma Rousseff, from the left-leaning Partido dos Trabalhadores (Workers' Party), as its first woman president. She is a former guerrilla leader and political prisoner, and her rise to Brazil's highest office opens a new chapter in Brazil's long political history. In October of 2014, in a very tight election, Rousseff was narrowly reelected to a second four-year term. She follows in the line of her political mentor (both hail from the same party), Lula da Silva, the former trade unionist, who led the country from 2002 until 2010.

The struggle for racial justice by Afro–civil society is the main concern of this book. From the 1930s until the middle of the 1970s, antiracist discourse and large-scale mobilization around racial justice was strictly limited in Brazil, first under the Estado Novo of the 1930s to 1945 and later during the military dictatorship from 1964 to 1985. During these two historical periods open and free discussions regarding racial issues, attempts at grassroots mobilization, and attempts to organize political parties not sanctioned by the state were censured and denounced as subversive. However, the reconstitution of formal democracy following military rule from 1964 to 1985, and the emergence of Afro-Brazilian social movements during the final years of the dictatorship, propelled a series of burning questions into Brazil's national discourse. Strong opposition to military rule peaked in the early 1970s, and by the end of the decade, the country had begun a process of liberalization that enabled a large cross-section of diverse groups to challenge political and economic inequality through social movement action. During the transition from military to civilian rule, Brazilian social movement groups sought to connect their struggle for democracy with their struggle for social justice (Andrews 1996). Issues of racial as well as gender equality emerged as important rallying cries for these new movements. Afro-Brazilians across the country joined labor leaders and church officials, as well as the rural and urban poor, and began an unprecedented dialogue on the role played by race and gender in structuring opportunities and rewards in Brazilian society (Lovell 2000).

Between 1974 and 1985 the process of political liberalization generated new space for racial contestation for Afro–social groups. An increasing number of Black movement groups and associations were formed in major cities across Brazil. Most were in Rio de Janeiro, São Paulo (Caldwell 2007), and Salvador. It was during this period that the seeds of a new civil society infrastructure were taking root and Afro–civil society began to emerge. The emergence of a Black and women's movement at this critical juncture played a key role in challenging centuries of racial and gender oppression. For example, the founding of the *blocos afros* (carnival groups) Ilê Aiyê and Olodum in Salvador in 1974 and 1979 respectively; the birth of the Sociedade de Intercâmbio Brasil-África (Society for Brazilian-African Exchange) and the Instituto de Pesquisas das Culturas Negras (Institute for the Study of Black Culture) in 1974 in Rio de Janeiro (Romo 2010, 260); and the emergence of the São Paulo–based Movimento Negro Unificado (Unified Black Movement) in 1978 as well as a number of other Black activist groups during the 1970s ushered in a new era of Black consciousness, Afro-referenced identities, social protest, and antiracist politics.

As new civic actors these Afro–nongovernmental organizations, groups, and associations arose outside the formal realm of the state as autonomous social agents for change, and their work was premised on antiracist strategies and grassroots mobilization. These groups are therefore broadly referred to as Afro–civil society throughout this book. The concept of civil society in Latin America (Alvarez, Dagnino, and Escobar 1998; Feinberg, Waisman, and Zamosc 2006; Stahler-Sholk, Vanden, and Becker 2014) forms the conceptual underpinning to understanding democracy, social and cultural citizenship, grassroots mobilization, identity constructions, and human rights: Afro–civil society builds on these novel conceptualizations by linking issues of racialization, modalities of Black consciousness, the repertoire of various Black identities, Black oppression, grassroots mobilization, and the Black struggle for human rights to the core of civil society in the Americas. In doing so, Afro–civil society challenges the normative underpinnings of traditional civil society while at the same time making it more conceptually and theoretically relevant to Black peoples and their forms of organization.

Throughout the 1980s there were also a significant number of Afro–civil society groups formed in Rio de Janeiro, São Paulo, Salvador, and other parts of the country. While race continued to be highly contested during the 1980s and 1990s, the emergence of civil society during the 1970s was pivotal, as it facilitated debates over the meaning of race by providing a social frame that was more conducive to the articulation of oppositional racial discourse (Caldwell 2007; Covin 2006). By 1988, Brazil was a de facto democracy, and the Black and women's movements, as well as other social groups, had become well established and serious political actors (Caldwell 2007, 159). Along with a new constitution, 1988 marked one hundred years since the formal abolition of slavery, and there were commemorative events across the country. Contributing to the rise of civil society were the process of political liberalization, a new constitution, and the formation of new Afro–social groups. This new constellation of forces provided the newly emergent Black movements a social license and new democratic space to raise a series of critical questions pertaining to racial discrimination and social inequality; it is argued that many of these questions had been texturally submerged for centuries.

One of the first—and perhaps thorniest—questions to emerge was about the nature of the structural racialized oppression and systemic racial discrimination faced by Afro-Brazilians; the second was about which grassroots strategies and mobilization tools to rally, organize, and educate the Afro-Brazilian masses regarding questions of racial and gender inequality were most appropriate; and the third was about what role the intersection of culture and politics played in shaping Afro-Brazilian consciousness and social identity, and, equally important, whether they could be used as platforms of mass-based social mobilization and grassroots action. These questions are of course linked to broader discourses pertaining to human rights and social citizenship because Afro-Brazilians were simultaneously de jure citizens but de facto noncitizens. Against this backdrop, it is argued that Brazil, and Salvador da Bahia in particular, offers an extremely compelling site of investigation based on the following:

1. Brazil has had a long and complex history of social discrimination. Brazilian history is marked by factors that shaped the Afro-Atlantic World—slavery, resistance, a slave culture, the formation of new identities, racism, and problems of integration (Butler 2000). These sociocultural practices—historically and currently—are deeply embedded in racialized and gendered hierarchies that are currently being dismantled and challenged by Afro–civil society groups all over the country and in Salvador in particular.

2. With an estimated 120 million people of African descent, Brazil has one of the largest African-descendant populations in the hemisphere (much larger than that of the United States). Africans arrived on Portuguese slave ships to toil in sugar plantations that made Brazil one of the richer colonies, and Salvador one of the richer cities, in the sixteenth and seventeenth centuries (Butler 2000). And while Blacks are found in most of Brazil's twenty-six states, Bahia and Salvador are largely recognized as a vibrant epicenter of Afro-Brazilian social identity and rich cultural traditions.

3. Brazil has recently enacted novel Black rights laws and legislation (antidiscrimination, affirmative action, and other measures). Brazil's affirmative action laws in education stand as some of the most comprehensive in all of the Americas (Hernández 2013). In 2012, the Brazilian Supreme Court issued a series of important rulings regarding affirmative action. These measures are uneven and are now being hotly debated by many different groups with different social, cultural, economic, and political interests.

4. Afro-Brazilian politicians are now represented on the local, regional, and national levels (Johnson 2000, 2008). The number of Blacks elected to political office over the past twenty-five years has risen slowly, but their overall numbers are extremely low both proportionately and in absolute numbers. In Salvador, Afro-Brazilian politicians are found at all levels of the local and regional government. However, formal Black politics in Salvador traverses a broad and diverse ideological spectrum, and Blacks are active in many different political parties that span from the most conservative to the most progressive.

The main questions this book seeks to address are the following: First, how are Afro-Brazilians (specifically in Salvador, Bahia) reconfiguring or challenging notions of citizenship, racialization, gender, territory, belonging, and national identities? Second, what is unique about the social, political, and cultural history of Salvador? Third, what are some of the key groups operating in Salvador, when did they emerge within the context of civil society, and what contributions have they made to Black social advancement? Finally, what are some of the key issues facing Afro–civil society groups and Black communities in Salvador, and how are they being addressed?

The main premise of this volume is that Afro-Brazilian civil society groups have matured since the 1970s and now are demanding and receiving some of the rights they were long denied and, at the same time, opening up new democratic spaces. This radical new space, it is argued, is the result of years of grassroots activism, political education, and mobilization across the country—and this new political transformation is rooted in concepts such as cultural citizenship, new citizenship, and active citizenship, each of which offers legitimation to claims of rights, space, and belonging in the dominant society. According to Blanca Silvestrini, these new forms of alternative citizenship refer to "the ways people organize their values, their beliefs about their rights, and their practices based on their sense of cultural belonging rather than on their formal status as citizens" (Silvestrini 1997, 44). The premise of this book is that by challenging and overturning racialized, gendered, and class structures, as well as by developing strategies of empowerment, Afro–social movements in Brazil are expanding citizenship and creating new democratic possibilities. Using Salvador as a case study, this book spotlights and explores the democratic challenges and possibilities for peoples of African descent in the Americas.

Theoretically, this research aims to contribute to Latin American critical racial theory and Black social movements by providing deep insights regarding cultural politics in Salvador, and to do so by exploring various forms of Black consciousness and cultural expressions, different levels of political action and social mobilization, and the role of Afro–civil society in relation to the state as well as by critically analyzing current debates on racial and gender discrimination and social inequality. Conceptually, this research seeks to break new ground by examining how Black politics (cultural and formal) are articulated and the ways in which the state is responding to various Black demands in Brazil, and particularly in Salvador da Bahia.

It is argued that over the past two decades African-descendants in

Brazil and Central and Latin America have been actively involved in the appropriation and articulation of Black identities for cultural and political ends. In many cases the assertion of Black identities in Afro-Latin communities and Salvador in particular has been closely tied to the increasing transnational circulation of Black cultural products and antiracist discourses. This study will amply demonstrate that Salvador da Bahia is emblematic of the articulation of new identities and antiracist discourses. The emergence of new forms of cultural politics in Black communities in Brazil and across Latin America necessitates the development of frameworks that examine the ways in which Afro-communities appropriate and articulate notions of Blackness (Gordon and Anderson 1999). It is argued that the construction and articulation of Afro-Brazilian identity in Bahia is inextricably linked to identity politics elsewhere in the African Diaspora in complex ways. In addition to Afro-Bahian cultural practices many Bahians of African descent also draw from increasingly globalized Afro-Diasporic discourses and practices as they construct and position their identities (Selka 2007, 135), and these discourses include narrative scripts on civil and human rights, police violence and criminal justice issues, affirmative action and education, Black cultural and formal politics, and economic survival; and the circuits for the articulation of Afro-Diasporic cultural formations include hip-hop, soul, reggae, slam poetry, and negritude, as well as cultural exchange programs, tourism, and transnational advocacy structures.

This study will place the global dimensions of Brazilians' racial formation in conversation with racial formations in other African Diasporic communities in the Spanish- and Portuguese-speaking Americas. Paul Gilroy defines Diaspora cultures as countercultures of modernity that share a common backdrop of experiences that include memory of slavery, legacies of Africanism, the effects of racism and discrimination, and dialogue and exchange with other Diaspora Black cultures (Gilroy 1993). While there is some comparative scholarship on race and racism focused on the United States and Brazil, works examining race and racism within a Diasporic frame are more recent and remain scarce. Dixon and Burdick's *Comparative Perspectives on Afro-Latin America* (2012) and Bernd Reiter and Kimberly Eison Simmons's

Afro-Descendants, Identity, and the Struggle for Development in the Americas (2012) are representative of the emerging new scholarship. Both volumes offer innovative theoretical perspectives on Black communities across the Americas from a comparative angle.

Regarding scholarship specific to Salvador, the works by Keisha-Khan Perry (2013), Scott Ickes (2013), Patricia Pinho (2010), and Stephen Selka (2007) offer extremely important ways of understanding state-sponsored racism and gender-structured social and urban moments (Perry 2013); the social history of Salvador and its emergence as a key site of Black identity and culture within Brazil (Ickes 2013); the social construction and complexity of Bahian identity and the role of the blocos (Pinho 2010); and the intersection of politics, religions, and Black identity (Selka 2007). This volume will enter into conversation with these works as it attempts to understand the emergence of Afro–civil society and Black politics.

Other works include those by Edmond Gordon and Mark Anderson (1999), who offer provocative discussions regarding the merits of focusing on the processes of racialization in the African Diaspora. They argue that a shift in focus that concentrates not so much on the essential features common to various peoples of African descent as on the various processes through which communities and individuals identify with one another highlights the central importance of race, racial formation, racial constructions, racial oppressions, and culture in making and remaking of Diaspora (Gordon and Anderson 1999). Moreover, situating racial formation in a Diasporic frame highlights similarities as well as differences in racialization processes in diverse national, social, and cultural contexts. It is argued that analyzing racial formation within a Diasporic context allows scholars to go beyond comparative approaches to racial formation by focusing on the transnational circulation of racist discourses and practices. Such an approach better frames our understanding of the ways in which hegemonic views of African Diasporic peoples have been premised on anti-Black discourses that privilege European-referenced identities, values, and cultural systems (Gordon and Anderson 1999).

Thematic Sections and Organization of Volume

This volume has seven chapters. The introduction provides a detailed theoretical overview of the study and situates the history of Black social movements and the rise of Black consciousness in a hemispheric framework. It highlights the rise of Black social movements in the Americas while underscoring the role of Black movements and mobilization.

Chapter 1 provides a brief discussion of the cultural history of Salvador da Bahia and the social landscape of contemporary Salvador. It also reviews key themes like cultural formations, identity, and the rise of cultural politics and formal politics. As one of the oldest sites in the Americas and the third-largest in city in Brazil, Salvador is vibrant, dynamic, and home to one of the largest, most politically active and diverse Black populations in the Americas.

Chapter 2 examines Salvador's relationship to the Portuguese colonial empire; the hierarchy of slavery; and the slave revolt of 1835, led by Muslim slaves, which was one of the most strategic slave insurrections in the Americas. The final section of the chapter deals with the abolition of slavery in 1888 and its consequences.

Chapter 3 charts the rise of burgeoning Salvador-specific Black social movements like the Afro-blocos Ilê Aiyê and Olodum. Chapter 4 focuses on the formation of the Movimento Negro Unificado in Salvador. Both chapters analyze how these groups burst onto the scene in the 1970s and how they radically reshaped Black cultural politics in Salvador and Brazil. Many of these movements were deemed "cultural" as they emphasized Afro-Diasporic music, religion, and identity as well as Black consciousness. At the same time, Black political movements in Rio de Janeiro, São Paulo, and Salvador emerged with an explicitly antiracist agenda. It is argued that these various movements laid the early foundations for Afro–civil society and were an engine for broader social change across Brazil and the Americas. Both chapters pay close attention to the rise of these early Afro-movements in Salvador as well as tease out many of the issues and debates they tackled during this time.

Chapters 5 and 6 address the controversial affirmative action laws recently enacted across Brazil. Starting in the middle of the 1990s Brazil passed a series of antidiscrimination laws, and one of the first was the Lei de Cotas Racias (Racial Quotas Bill), which implements a quota system for Blacks and indigenous students in Brazilian federal universities. The year 2012 was a watershed for affirmative action in Brazil, as there were a series of laws and constitutional rulings that turbocharged Afro–civil society and Black social movements. In April of 2012, the Supremo Tribunal Federal (Brazilian Supreme Court) ruled 10–0 in favor of affirmative action regarding admission policies at the University of Brasília and the University of Rio do Sol. In May of 2012, the Supremo Tribunal Federal, in another very important legal case, ruled in favor of a federal scholarship program aimed at Black and indigenous students. Some movement activists believe that these are some of the most important recent Supreme Court decisions that address historical wrongs. Along with these two legal victories, in August of 2012, President Dilma Rousseff signed the Law of Social Quotas, which requires all federal universities to reserve at least 40 percent of their seats for Black and indigenous students. Current discussions about affirmative action, racial quotas, and racial discrimination are at a fever pitch, as they are being hotly debated across the country. Since affirmative action was one of the principal demands of Black movement groups, these decisions, at least on the surface, appear to be victories. However, there are many currents within these debates that need to be teased out. This chapter will untangle and situate these debates within the broader racial discourses (historical and contemporary) and struggle for social justice in Brazil.

Chapter 6 builds on chapter 5 by providing an in-depth discussion of the rise of debates surrounding affirmative action specific to Salvador, concentrating on the Steve Biko Cultural Institute and Pré-vestibular para Negros e Carentes Movimento (Pre-vestibular for Blacks and the Poor Movement). It contextualizes the history and role of Black groups and their efforts to place affirmative action on the table as a serious issue. This chapter spotlights the struggle over affirmative action (implementation and enactment) and the central role played by Afro–civil society groups in Salvador.

The final chapter offers a contextual view into the opaque world of Brazilian and Salvadoran politics. Regrettably, there are few studies on Black formal politics in Brazil and Afro–Latin America; however, political scientists over the last two decades have started to make more inroads and focus more on this under-researched and overlooked field. Political scientists like Michael Hanchard (1994), Ollie Johnson (1998, 2000, 2008), Bernd Reiter (2009, 2010), Cloves Luiz Oliveira (1997, 2010), Kwame Dixon (2008, 2012), Gladys L. Mitchell (2009, 2010), and others have made important contributions to understanding Black consciousness and social movements, the lack of Black political power in Latin America, the rise of Black candidates in congressional and senate races, Black voting habits in Latin America, and the intersection of race and politics. However, more studies are desperately needed that focus on racialized social hierarchies and forms of racial inequality that exclude and deny Afro-groups opportunities in political systems. Chapter 7 analyzes the rise of Black electoral power in Brazil and Salvador from the 1980s to the present.

The Political and Social Landscape of Salvador da Bahia

Salvador da Bahia (hereinafter referred to as Salvador) is unique and exceptional, as it stands at the rugged cross-sections of a vibrant transnational Black identity, contested local grassroots politics, and strong African-referenced cultural formations. The city of Salvador is located in the state of Bahia on the northeastern coast of Brazil, south of Recife and north of Rio de Janeiro. Its official name is São Salvador da Bahia de Todos os Santos. Many people, however, refer to the city of Salvador as Bahia. It should be noted that Salvador is the city whereas Bahia is the state even though they are used synonymously. The state of Bahia was at one time the most prosperous sugar-producing region in the New World (Reis 1993). Salvador was the first capital of Brazil and remained so until 1763, when it was succeeded by Rio de Janeiro and eventually Brasília, the current capital of Brazil.

Bahia's strategic importance and place within Brazil has ebbed and flowed over time: its earlier colonial preeminence collapsed in the eighteenth century, but it made a slight recovery in the last half of the twentieth century. As the Portuguese began to import African slaves to labor in the ever-growing sugar industry, Salvador became the port of entry for a steady stream of slave labor. During this time sugar plantations based mainly on slave labor financed the development of a profitable export market as well as a wealthy slave-owning class. However, the economy bottomed out as world sugar prices declined dramatically due to increased sugar production in other parts of the Americas (Romo 2010).

The northeastern corner of Brazil, where the state of Bahia is located, is one of the poorest regions in Brazil (Love and Baer 2009). Salvador is the third-largest city in Brazil (followed by Rio and São Paulo), and according to the Brazilian Institute of Geography and Statistics, the population was estimated to be 2,710,968 people for the year 2012. The average salary in Brazil/Salvador was R$678 (US$339) in January 1, 2013. This amount represents an increase of 9 percent compared to the previous year of 2012, R$670 (US$335). The daily salary is R$22.60 (US$11.30) and the hourly wage is R$3.08 (US$1.54) (Instituto Brasileiro de Geografia e Estatística / Brazilian Institute of Geography and Statistics 2014).

The city of Salvador is majestic and beautiful, and its bold colonial-style architecture stands out as one of the best architectural treasures in the Americas according to UNESCO. The city is defined by its long, snaking coastline, its white, sandy beaches, and its natural sand dunes, which attract thousands of local and international tourists each year. Salvador is oftentimes referred to as the Roma Negra, or Black Rome, of the Americas, because it is seen as being a harbor for African-based cultural traditions like Candomblé (an Afro-Brazilian religion) and *capoeira* (a type of martial art that originated in Angola) as well as other New World Afro–cultural productions. In fact Salvador is considered the cradle of Afro-Brazilian culture and the homeland of Candomblé (Selka 2007). It is a cultural jewel and is considered a mecca for Africans in the Diaspora, and on any given day its streets overflow with vibrant Black cultural life, performances by renowned Black artists, theater performances, open-air capoeira demonstrations, arts and crafts, and a rich tapestry of African-influenced culture throughout the city. Given Salvador's (and Bahia's) large Black population and its Afro-referenced cultural formation, it is considered a vibrant center of racial consciousness and political activism across Brazil and throughout the African Diaspora.

Afro-Bahian–referenced cultural productions include Candomblé and capoeira as well as other Afro-rooted art forms such as reggae, hip-hop, Black poetry and spoken word, and Black theater and dance. Candomblé is an Afro-Brazilian religion and is one of the most popular in Brazil. It roots lie in West Africa, the home of the *orixás*, spiritual forces who exist on planes superior to that of humans. According to Rachel Harding, Candomblé is a rich, poetic, complex cosmology and set of rituals, with deep and obvious roots in several religious traditions of West and Central Africa. It incubated within the specific matrixes of slavery, colonialism, and mercantilism that characterized Brazil from the sixteenth century to the present (Harding 2000).

Capoeira is an Afro-Brazilian martial art form and is largely believed to have originated in parts of Angola. Capoeira consists of small cadres of dancers, called *capoeiristas*, moving about in slow, unpredictable circles like wrestlers who without notice quickly catapult themselves upside down, standing on their hands in acts that seem to defy gravity as they simultaneously rotate their feet in a series of balancing and counterbalancing moves. Judith Butler argues that both Candomblé and capoeira provide alternative communities and serve as power bases while offering alternative spaces to subvert elite attempts to impose a hegemonic view on Bahian society (Butler 2000). These Afro-Bahian cultural productions now serve as crucial circuits in the transmission and dissemination of Afro-Bahian and Brazilian national culture. In other words they are now codified and embedded as central to and integral parts of Brazilian national and regional social identity. The process of "Afro-referenced identity commodification" by the state (local, regional, and national) must be understood as a long, uneven, contradictory process that began unfolding in roughly the middle part of the twentieth century (Ickes 2013). By the 1970s capoeira was officially classified as folklore by the city of Salvador, and while Afro-referenced culture in Bahia may now be in vogue and trendy, this was not always the case.

In Salvador historically and to some extent today, the most significant barrier to increased social standing is the open embrace of African cultural practices, as the local white ruling elite have long believed them to be dangerous and a form of counter-modernity. During Brazil's First Republic from 1889 to 1930 (slavery was officially abolished in 1888) the mainly white Bahian elite feared that Brazil's

African-descended population prevented or at least delayed the country's reaching the level of progress Europe and the United States had achieved (Ickes 2013). Roughly twenty-five years after the abolition of slavery, members of Salvador's ruling white elite fought to eliminate and socially "cleanse" the city's public life of African culture.

At the dawn of the twentieth century, scientific racism largely ruled the day, and it framed how the Bahian elite saw African culture (Ickes 2013). Race "science" was used to argue that Blacks were less intelligent, dangerous, and of course more prone to extreme criminal behavior. Using the "science of the day," the ruling elite along with the press and the police specifically targeted Black culture. African-remnant culture in food and language, public events like carnival, and popular religious practices such as Candomblé and capoeira were demonized in the press. Candomblé was seen as dangerous "black magic," barbaric, and a threat to public health. Capoeira was defined as a brutally shiftless practice undertaken by a lazy yet menacing underclass and was considered a threat to local authorities. By 1905 African carnival clubs' themes and costumes were officially banned (Ickes 2013). In particular, from the early years of the 1900s until roughly the 1920s, practitioners of Candomblé were patrolled, repressed, and terrorized by the police and other institutions of the state.

However, by the 1930s there were a set of new forces at play that radically repositioned the value of African Bahian cultural contributions. The revitalization of African Bahian cultures during the 1930s and after had its roots in five separate but interrelated spheres: first, the politics of the Gertulio Vargas (1930 to 1954), whose policies promoted Brazilian popular culture and African Bahian culture in particular (Ickes 2013, 5); second, the writings of Brazilian intellectuals Gilberto Freyre, Arthur Ramos, Edison Carneiro, and many others who established important new markers for understanding and appreciating African cultures (Romo 2010, 61); third, the scholarly productions of foreign intellectuals, mainly anthropologists like Ruth Landes, Donald Pierson, Melville Herskovits, Roger Bastides, and sociologist Franklin Frazier, who all but in different ways made important contributions to investigating and understanding Afro-Bahian culture in the 1940s and 1950s (Romo 2010, 113); fourth, the UNESCO studies of the 1950s (Romo

2010); and fifth and perhaps most important, the role played by Candomblé leaders in reasserting their cultural agency. As a result of these interrelated processes, according to historian Scott Ickes, Bahia now occupies a place of honor and privilege within the African Diaspora (Ickes 2013).

However such privilege and honor comes at a steep price. Currently, Afro-Bahian culture is so "hot" that some argue that it is being manipulated, exploited, and mass-marketed simultaneously by different sectors for various reasons—first by some Black identity groups who have formed partnerships with local elites, and second by sectors of Bahia's elite who have invested heavily in the concept of *baianidad* (Afro-Bahian culture), namely local political institutions and the tourism-industrial complex. Patricia Pinho refers to this as "milking mama Africa" (Pinho 2010, 9). In other words, the expedient use of Black culture and the exchange of favors carried out between key sectors of Bahian society have "milked mother Africa," exploiting Black cultural productions instead of fighting racial inequality (Pinho 2010, 10).

Salvador's cultural nerve center, Pelourinho (the name of a whipping post where slaves were beaten), is in the historic center and is considered a unique cultural and architectural treasure. It was declared a World Heritage Site by UNESCO in 1985. Many foreigners came to know Pelourinho in 1996 when its majestic colonial buildings served as the backdrop to Michael Jackson's now-famous video "They Don't Care about Us." Usually defined by its stunning seventeenth- and eighteenth-century colonial architecture, bright colorful churches, and narrow cobblestone streets, for many who know its past history, Pelourinho is a grim reminder of its disturbing colonial and brutal slave history.

Pelourinho, however, is a unique cultural heritage site, and Afro-Bahian cultural productions are now central to Salvador's local, regional, and transnational cultural identity, as they are structurally linked to both the political economy of tourism and the larger forces of commodification. In Pelourinho there are high-end restaurants, souvenir shops, cafés, bookstores, and *pousadas* (bed-and-breakfast inns) located alongside nongovernmental organizations and cultural groups. Real estate and developmental plans and the forces of tourism have contributed to skyrocketing prices and increased property values. Currently, many of the longtime local residents, the majority of whom are poor and Black, are fighting to stay in their homes as residential property and land values have increased exponentially. Their struggles, as well as those of other local communities in Salvador, will be fleshed out, as they serve to underscore some of the other local urban struggles unfolding across Salvador.

As a predominantly Black city with such recognized Afro–cultural productions, Salvador has become a key site and exchange for many Afro–North Americans, Europeans, and Japanese seeking to explore Afro-Diasporic identity, religion, music, politics, and sexuality. Salvador thus represents a powerful representation of a specific transnational Afro-Diasporic cultural and social identity. Patricia Pinho (2010), Stephen Selka (2007), Keisha-Khan Perry (2013), and others convincingly argue that Bahia is now an important center in the Black Atlantic World and that in the last two decades it has become an important reference for the development of Black identities constructed in other points of the Diaspora (Pinho 2010). Bahia's vibrant Black culture is tied to several hegemonic processes: a Disaporic Black social consciousness, Afro-referenced identities, and Black cultural formations mitigated via the local and transnational tourism (or the tourism-industrial complex).

Building on works by Kim Butler (2000), Ollie Johnson (2008, 2013), Stephen Selka (2007), Patricia Pinho (2010), Anedelia Romo (2010), Paulina Alberto (2011), Cheryl Sterling (2012), Keisha-Khan Perry (2013), Scott Ickes (2013), John Burdick (2013), and others, this study examines the process of Black identity commodification, the intersection of Black grassroots mobilization, religion, formal and informal politics, their relation to identity, and the role of nongovernmental organizations and Afro–civil society in constructing new Black politics and political structures. The main argument is that Salvador's cultural productions and social identities are now linked to national and transnational commercial ventures and must be understood against this backdrop. However, despite their unique cultural productions, the relative strength of Afro–civil society, their strong Afro-referenced Black consciousness, and an active Black political intelligentsia, Blacks in Salvador have made only modest political gains (municipal and state level), and more disturbing is that the majority of Blacks in Bahia still live in deep, abject, and grinding poverty. Along these lines there are several competing constructions of Salvador: one version is neatly constructed and presented as the "Black Rome," which underscores its vibrant cultural formation and its unique Blackness; the other version is one that emphasizes the endemic violence at play across Salvador as well as the marginal status of the "dangerous" poor Black masses who occupy "dark urban spaces" in the inner city, periphery, and favelas. These competing social constructions of Salvador must first be properly contextualized and then deconstructed in order to better grasp and understand modern Black Salvador's social identity and its long, tortured history.

"Dark urban space" according to Harding has unarticulated locational possibilities because its meaning shifts and mutates across time and space. In Salvador, the spaces assigned to Blacks historically and currently are at the lowest possible level of social stratification; that is, the "street," or the favela, a certain neighborhood, the color or shade of one's skin, a particular religious practice (Catholicism, Protestantism, or Candomblé), or one's location in the labor market—to name only a few—define Black social space in Salvador (Harding 2000, xvii). The marginal "social spaces" that Blacks currently occupy in Salvador (and the state of Bahia) are more astounding because Salvador is home to one of the largest, most visible, and most politically active Black populations in the Americas, with a vast network of civil society and vibrant social movements and groups working on a number of important social justice issues. Some of these issues include housing, education, health, land rights (rural and urban), electoral and grassroots politics, women's rights, gay, lesbian, transsexual, and transgender issues, and many more. Yet, despite its cultural and social richness and active Black social movements, the Afro-Bahian population has some of the highest rates of poverty, unemployment and underemployment, and violence in the country, including both police and other forms of daily violence. Additionally, Bahia (the state) and Salvador (the city) are two of the poorest regions in Brazil, characterized by high levels of income inequality. And, despite having a majority Black and politically active population, Salvador's political and economic structures remain to this day de facto mainly white. In this scenario Afro–cultural productions and the image of Bahia are used as a cultural magnet to draw attention to Salvador by attracting tourist dollars, and such relations are facilitated by the tourism industry with the aid of local and state authorities as well as some Black groups, while the majority of Blacks in Salvador receive little or no benefit from such relations.

On some level members of the local Black commercial elite and sectors of the Black tourism industry have formed a partnership to promote Afro-Bahian cultural productions. As Pinho and others point out, the most problematic aspect of the relationship is not the exploitation of Black cultural formations per se but rather how they are de-linked from the broader questions of racial justice (or injustice). In fact most visitors who come to Salvador or Pelourinho have no idea of its knotty racial history or that the majority of the urban poor live in deep, grinding poverty, which is of course out of view and not part of the mainstream tourist circuits. This study therefore aims to provide a frame as well as address these contradictions by examining the rise of Black social movements, grassroots politics, and Afro–civil society in Salvador.

Over the past decade, Blacks have, however, made slow inroads and have been elected to local, state, and federal office. But the representation of Afro-Brazilians on the local, state, and regional level is extremely low. In order to understand this thorny problem the tense interplay of past and current forms of marginalization and disenfranchisement, as well as the long history of racial discrimination in both Salvador and Brazil, will be teased out. The fact that Blacks have been unable to gain a modicum of political power within Salvador (and the state of Bahia)—and across Brazil—still confounds many observers. And regrettably there are no easy or simple answers as to why Blacks in Salvador (and the state of Bahia) have not been able to harness their numbers into effective political power.

However, hidden in plain view are the deep Black cultural politics operating in Salvador, as Blacks have been more active outside the realm of formal politics. Given their exclusion from the formal political sphere Blacks have been forced to create new forms and structures for participation. With the emergence of blocos afros such as Ilê Aiyê and Olodum (Altino de Souza 2006), Black mobilization groups such as Movimento Negro Unificado (MNU) in the 1970s, and other Black groups like the Steve Biko Cultural Institute in the 1990s, we witness two complementary and interwoven processes: first, the development of new forms of Black cultural politics in Brazil and Salvador; second, the rise of new Black social consciousness with links to Black transnational advocacy networks in the Americas and Africa. The founding of the blocos afros and MNU during this period signaled the emergence of a new form of antiracist discourse, resistance, and hegemonic opposition as well as new forms of radical Black social consciousness.

In Salvador starting in the 1970s a vibrant cross-section of groups like the blocos afros as part of cultural movements, the MNU, the Steve Biko Cultural Institute, a diverse section of university students, various neighborhood associations, Black trade union leaders, Black members of the Partido dos Trabalhadores (Workers' Party) and other political parties, and religious leaders cultivated new forms of discourse through political education, music, dance, and art. There was in fact a rearticulation of Black identities as a conscious political strategy, serving as a platform to create a radical new Black politics informed by references to Africa, Afro-Diasporic identity, slavery, race, and racism, while at the same time validating Afro-Brazilian cultural and aesthetic formations. More importantly, these groups spoke directly to the marginalization and social exclusion of Blacks within Salvadoran and Brazilian society.

The founding of the two blocos afros, Ilê Aiyê and Olodum (1974 and 1979 respectively in Salvador), and the formation of the MNU cell in Salvador in the late 1970s (MNU was first organized in São Paulo in 1978) were important historical markers. There were other trailblazing groups, such as the Steve Biko Cultural Institute, founded in 1992, which served to enrich debates pertaining to Black identity, Black education, the quality of education, and affirmative action. Named after the South African, antiapartheid, human rights activist, the Steve Biko Cultural Institute was created to provide educational opportunities to socially excluded Afro-Brazilian youth, as well as to prepare them for Brazil's notoriously difficult college entrance exam, known as the

FIGURE 1.1. A poster advertising a popular music festival organized by the bloco Olodum. In possession of author.

vestibular (college entrance exam). The Steve Biko Cooperative (it later changed its name) would also be an early proponent in some of the debates on affirmative action as it challenged the low number of Black students and professors in Bahia's two main universities. Similar to the Brazilian educator Paulo Freire, who sought to radically transform education, the founders of Biko wanted to not only cultivate a critical consciousness but also take it a step further by framing education within a critical Black radical consciousness connected to history, politics, and culture.

Additionally, the founding in Salvador of Centro Arquidiocensano de Articulação da Pastoral Afro (CAAPA) in 1999 (Selka 2007, 34), rooted in ideas of liberation theology—whose stated goal is to address racism and the underrepresentation of Blacks within the church, raise Black consciousness, dialogue with the Candomblé community, and reaffirm Afro-Brazilian identity—represented another historical marker in Salvador (Selka 2007, 35).

Simultaneously there were other historically specific and important cultural formations operating, such as Candomblé and capoeira, but it was groups like the blocos afros, MNU, Steve Biko, and to some extent the early Black militants of the Workers' Party that challenged Afro-Brazilians to think more critically about Black identity, Black culture, and Black politics in new conceptual dimensions. These groups as well as their origins, histories, and how they contributed to the rise of

Afro–civil society and Black cultural politics in Salvador will be dealt with and placed within the frame of the cultural politics of Salvador. My main premise is that in order to comprehend modern Salvador as a unique cultural space it is absolutely critical to understand the emergence of Afro–civil society and the rise of radical Black cultural politics in the 1970s. The central argument is that Black culture, accumulated over several centuries, intervened in the operation, mitigation, and facilitation of political power, however unevenly. In this context cultural struggles are inherently political because meanings are constitutive of processes that seek to transform or preserve hegemonic relations.

Seen through this lens and against this backdrop, Afro–social movements in Salvador have been and are engaged in several important cultural projects that are inherently political: first, they are constructing new forms of citizenship by claiming new rights; second, they are examining, evaluating, and testing recently enacted antidiscrimination and affirmative action measures; third, they are struggling to regain or reclaim land rights both rural and urban; and fourth, they are seeking to increase political participation and representation on the local, state, and federal levels. In doing so, Afro–civil society groups in Salvador are challenging the dominant hegemony by seeking to alter historically inscribed forms of discrimination and destabilize centuries-old racialized social hierarchies.

Given its thorny history of racialization, Salvador therefore serves as a crucial site of social, political, and cultural investigation, standing at the cross-section of Afro transnational Diasporic culture, grassroots advocacy, vibrant Afro–civil society, and contested local, state, and national politics. Along these lines Afro-groups in Brazil and Salvador are involved in a series of specific hegemonic contestations and negotiations involving social identity, cultural formations, the fight to secure and maintain land and territories, and the struggle for citizenship and human rights.

Social Identity and Black Struggles in Brazil

Black social identities and their multiple social constructions are central to understanding the struggles of Afro-Brazilians for inclusion, equality, and democracy. First, Afro-Brazilian Black social identities are not fixed and static but fluid and dynamic; second, it is useful to think about multiple and overlapping or intersectional identities with the history of slavery, racism, racialization, racial violence, social class, gender, religion, skin color, oppression, and memory of Africa as some of the core elements structuring Afro-Brazilian identities; third, identity is texturally and socially linked to power, however unequally. Within this matrix there are simultaneously competing and contradictory representations of what it means to be Black in Brazil and more specifically in Bahia by both Blacks and non-Blacks, Brazilians and non-Brazilians. Selka argues that within these competing forms of representation it is also crucial to consider how such representations might influence mobilization efforts in the Black movement (Selka 2007).

In Bahia, debates about the formation of Afro-Brazilian identity tend to center on struggles over religion (Candomblé, Catholicism, or Protestantism), racial classification (Black or *negro*, brown or *moreno*), social class (working versus middle class), spatial (rural versus urban), and other identity platforms. Moreover, according to Selka, identity-based approaches must include a better understanding of identity: that it is not simply an expedient means for social mobilization but is premised on the fundamental need for recognition, that the interests of a particular group are not given but constructed through discursive practices, and that social movements are not homogenous but complex and shifting networks of discourses and practices (Selka 2007, 134). Black identity and social consciousness in Salvador (and Brazil) therefore are understood within a broad repertoire of social relations as political and politicized. Accepting and affirming Black identity is not simply a demand for rights and social inclusion but a specific demand to be fully recognized and accepted as Black and simultaneously engage in politics and cultural practices around such constructions. In short, being Black and poor and therefore marginal in Brazil is political and politicized, as these are relations of power that reflect social inequality and a long history of racial discrimination.

In particular, discourses over racial classification (negro, *mulato*, and moreno) have served as forms of subordination and contestation simultaneously. Afro-Brazilians and other Black populations in the Americas have had to negotiate and renegotiate their identities via a series of hegemonic projects ranging from *mestiçagem* or *mestizaje* and "racial democracy" to current forms of multiculturalism. As Selka and Perry note, any project examining Afro-Brazilian identity must engage both the discourses of mestiçagem, which tends to undermine the foundations for strong Black identity, and the need for a more radical politics (Selka 2007, 121). In this hegemonic scenario African and Black identity were often seen as negative, and Afro-Brazilians thus sought creative strategies to reposition themselves via the prevailing hegemonic discourses. According to Kim Butler, since the early twentieth century Afro-Brazilians have employed ethnicity as a strategy of social and political advancement: "The development of empowering ethnic identities became a critical avenue for a people systematically denied that power by the societies in which they lived" (Butler 2000, 49). Afro-Brazilian social identity and cultural formations are complementary processes (religion, dance, food), and both were often devalued, dehumanized, and pushed to the lowest level of social hierarchies. Across time and space and based on the prevailing political hegemony, cultural formations such as Candomblé and capoeira were sometimes outlawed or discouraged and at other times highly valued or commodified if they could be coopted for commercial ventures or manipulated by the state for its own narrow purposes.

The issue of land and territory is also crucial to understanding the social history of Afro-Brazil and Afro-Bahia in particular, as they are deeply rooted and linked to Afro-Brazilian social identity and cultural practices. Afro-Brazilians were once slaves and thus had intimate connections with the land and territory and this is of course still the case today. Afro-Brazilians have often been excluded or denied land ownership and tenure and forcefully evicted from their lands. Currently in Salvador in both rural and urban settings, contentious battles are being waged by poor constituencies as they seek to claim or maintain lands they have occupied for decades or centuries. Keisha-Khan Perry's research underscores the tense urban land struggles unfolding across Salvador, and she emphasizes how Blackness and class are articulated within a gender matrix. Black movements in Brazil have struggled since the early 1980s to build a movement to influence state policy grounded in a gender-articulated politics. Perry's (2013) research focuses on the community of Gamboa de Baixo (a working-class community located in Salvador). In this research, she constructs a gendered analysis of Afro-women's grassroots urban politics that articulates racial and class-based claims to urban space and in doing so makes an important contribution to Afro-Brazilian social movements and forms of urban resistance.

Her research explores state-sponsored racism and violence toward Blacks in the forced demolition of urban neighborhoods and the relocation of Blacks to the periphery of the city. Her analysis amply illustrates how Black women's resistance to displacement, eviction, and discriminatory urban practices in Salvador occurs on a racialized and gendered terrain of domination as well as how Black women's resistance unites class, space, and gender politics (Perry 2013, 12). Building on the work of Perry and others, this research will demonstrate the power of Black mobilizations in Salvador that are intersectional and multidimensional and that this power results from their ability to provide a synthesis of Black identity rooted in race, class, and gender.

The city of Salvador—structurally unequal, racialized, and gendered—operates based on an urban racialized spatial logic, and the city's urban development plans are a public airing of the sharp power differentials that have defined social relations between the poor Black majority and whites, between the rich and the poor (Perry 2013, 221). In Salvador and in its periphery as well as across Brazil there are a series of events that have only exacerbated underlying social tensions and land issues. Mega-events such as the Federations Cup (summer 2013) brought hundreds of thousands of people—including many in Salvador—to the streets as they protested not only the games but the massive amounts of money spent on stadiums (Goodman 2013). Moreover, mega-events like the World Cup (2014) and the Olympic Games (in the summer of 2016 Rio de Janeiro will host the Olympics) have opened new wounds and exposed fragile fault lines over land, housing, public transportation, roads, security, health, and police issues in Salvador, Rio de Janeiro, and São Paulo (and other cities) between poor

FIGURE 1.2. Social protest against the World Cup in Salvador in the summer of 2013: "From the World Cup I want more, I want transportation, health, and housing." Photo by author.

FIGURE 1.3. Social protest against the World Cup in Salvador in the summer of 2013: "We don't want Stadiums nor the World Cup." Photo by author.

urban dwellers, local and regional governments, and powerful real estate interests.

Urban revitalization plans in the center of Salvador during recent decades have consisted of the violent demolition of homes and mass expulsion and displacement of residents to the city's periphery (Perry 2013). In Salvador, urban struggles against discrimination have emerged to dismantle discrimination against Black people (Butler 2000). Poor, Black urban dwellers in communities like Barrio da la Paz (located on the northern periphery of Salvador) and Gamboa de Baixo (located in the center) and the working poor who reside in the historic center of Pelourinho are jittery as they live under the daily threat of forced eviction and expulsion from their homes. These mega-events and powerful real estate interests have opened a new chapter in the fight over urban spaces in Salvador. The communities of Barrio da Paz, Pelourinho, and Gamboa da Baixo as well as other similarly situated communities in Salvador are the new flash points of twenty-first-century urban struggles. These struggles serve as important markers for this book.

The main focus of this investigation revolves around the axis of African social identity, culture, land, religion, and territory; it is argued that they are directly linked to social citizenship and human rights and represent hegemonic constructions. These hegemonic constructions are conceptualized as rooted in complex layers, textures, and nuances that define many aspects of the daily life experiences of Afro-Brazilians. Many Afro-Brazilians have struggled to be included as real citizens with rights and duties while being pushed to the lowest levels of society. The main argument of this book is threefold: first, Afro-Brazilians are active agents of social change because they challenge the dominant hegemonies; second, they have been denied basic human rights, and their current struggle is for social and cultural identity, land and territories, and full and equal citizenship and human rights protections; third, Salvador represents a rich case study and a compelling site for this investigation and research as it mirrors many of the struggles Afro-descendants face across Brazil and the Americas.

Slavery in Salvador

There were no historians, anthropologists, or social scientists aboard the slave ships as they crossed the Atlantic, nor did any toil on the plantations, and none were involved in or planned the slave revolts and insurrections so well documented in the literature. Invariably this is a serious problem in our attempt to form a sophisticated understanding of formations, identities, and life patterns of slave communities over the past few centuries. The small fraction of what we think we know about plantation slavery in the Americas emerges from a rough patchwork of fragmented ideas, conjectures, and uneven theories woven together over last few hundred years or so. Fragments of this fissured and tormented history emerge from tiny threads of history in the form of slave accounts and narratives, plantation owners' records and observations, slaver and shipper records, travel logs, and of course scholarly papers, studies, and books. What we do know for certain is that slavery and slave life was extremely harsh and brutal and a perfectly dehumanizing social experience—and is perhaps on some level beyond the grasp of our social imagination (Degler 1972; Conrad 1972; Hasenbalg 1984). Along with emphasizing the brutality of the slave experience many studies emphasize slave rebellions and *quilombos* (maroon communities composed of Afro-Brazilians who fled slavery and remained free) (Schwartz 1992; Reis 1993).

According to Stuart Schwartz, Brazil almost from its origin as a European colony in 1500 until it finally abolished slavery in 1888 wove the strands of coerced labor, commercial capitalism, and Iberian seigniorial traditions and attitudes into a complex fabric. Such a process resulted in a multiracial, stratified society profoundly influenced by the plantation system. Slavery, it is argued, must be viewed as part of the larger social structures refracting economic and social relations (Schwartz 1986). Therefore, in order to comprehend Brazil and Salvador one must have some understanding of the role of slavery and how it defined the political economy, racial categories, cultural formations, national identity, and the infinite possible variations that can result from these relationships. In short slavery and slave life is central to understanding modern Brazil and Bahia.

Portuguese state policy made Black slavery the foundation of Brazil's social and economic order during three centuries of colonial rule (Andrews 1988), and slave labor occupied a key position within the plantation economy. According to the conservative estimates of Phillip Curtin almost four million African slaves arrived to the slave markets of Brazil from the mid-1600s until the nineteenth century. These numbers are of course staggering, and almost 1.5 million were brought to the shores of Bahia. Most were young men between the ages of sixteen and thirty (Curtin 1969). In 1823, it is estimated, the province of Bahia had 20 percent of all Brazilian slaves (Klein 1986, 66).

The social history of Afro-Brazil must be understood from several vantage points. Brazil and the Afro-Atlantic slavery that brought Africans to Brazil were part of an important global trade network that centered on Portugal, Africa, and Asia. During this time slaves and sugar among other commodities were the motor force that fueled Portuguese colonialism. Bahia emerged as one of the crucial links to the Black Atlantic during the colonial period when the transatlantic slave trade placed Brazil inside the network of international commerce. At one time during the colonial period, Salvador was Brazil's largest and most important city, given its strategic location on the northeastern coast, where it served as a key route in the Portuguese transnational empire. Salvador was a major slave port, and the surrounding area formed the backbone of the traditional sugar-based plantation economy.

Starting in 1549 until 1763, Bahia was the colonial capital of Brazil as well as the capital of Portuguese America, but in recognition of the growing economic and strategic importance of the South the Brazilian capital was transferred to Rio de Janeiro, which emerged as the major port of slaves, mainly from Angola (Nishida 2003, 15).

Salvador was also seat of the governor-general viceroyalty, the royal treasury, and the high court, and later its economy became a major port for the export of sugar and tobacco in the eighteenth century (Nishida 2003, 13). By the nineteenth century, Salvador, whose population had grown from fifty thousand to nearly two hundred thousand, was the economic and political center of Brazil. During this time Salvador displayed all of the elements of a major regional political and economic powerhouse: opulent merchant families dealing in sugar exports, African slaves, and well-connected sugar and commercial interests with administrative and judicial links to the Brazilian empire (Kraay 1998, 4). The colonial wealth and prosperity of Salvador was produced squarely on the backs of slave and free workers who labored in the cane fields and sugar mills. Slave history and hierarchy in Salvador is of course extremely complex. According to Nishida, urban slavery developed and existed in Salvador and throughout the city, and people of African descent have constituted a majority from the early colonial times to the present (Nishida 2003). She further argues that the city of Salvador provides a provocative site for rich discussions on the creation of identity during the slave regime (Nishida 2003). The identity construction process of the slave regime played a critical role in defining and constructing Afro-Brazilian identity, and these constructs would serve as the basis of structuring modern Brazilian identity both Black and white.

There were several criteria that determined a person's rank in Brazil during this time. In Salvador the population of African descent was divided into two categories based on the place of birth (African-born and Brazilian-born Blacks) and into three categories in terms of legal status—slave (*escravo*), ex-slave (*forro* or *libretto*), and freeborn (*livre*). Therefore, place of birth and labor status were important markers as well as ethnicity and, later, skin tone. Blacks born in Brazil were referred to as *crioulo*; there were *cabras*, whose color was somewhere between that of Blacks and mulatos, sometimes referred to as *pardo*; and Brazilian-born Blacks were distinguished from African Blacks, with Africans referred to as *prêtos*. Africans were also designated by their ethnicities or nations (Angola, Nigeria). Equally important is that Africans and Afro-Bahians could be freeborn, slave, or freed, and the ex-slave's freedom did not mean absolute equality with the freeborn (Reis 1993, 5).

This system of complex classification also applied to whites, as there were whites who were Portuguese and "white" born in Brazil; usually the Portuguese whites were higher in status and rank. In Salvador the social construction of racial and ethnic categories is central to understanding the period from 1800 to 1888, when slavery was finally abolished. Historian Mieko Nishida highlights several important time frames to see the transformation in African and Black identity in Salvador from 1808 to roughly 1888. There are four main periods to consider. During the first period from 1808 to 1830, African-born persons constituted the majority of the city's population. Africans from *nação* (nations) were identified based on where they were thought to have originated in Africa. "Mina" signified someone from Angola and "Nagô" (Oyo, Yoruba) identified someone from the region of Nigeria. These groups formed their own associations and Brazilians of all colors were excluded (Nishida 2003, 365).

The second period, from 1831 to 1850, began with the increase of Brazilian-born Blacks (*crioulos*) in the population and the creation of their own institutions. During this period an interethnic African identity was emerging and it began to slowly blur the boundaries between African-born and native-born Blacks. In the third stage, 1851 to 1870, Pan-African identity was solidified with a greater reliance on personal networks than on professional organizations (Nishida 2003, 365).

In the last stage, between 1871 and 1888, Brazilian-born mulatos (light-skinned Blacks) came to outnumber Blacks for the first time in Salvador's history (Nishida 2003, 25). These transformations reflected how categories of color (prêto and pardo) now replaced old labels denoting nationality such as crioulo (Nishida 2003, 25). In short, Africans were becoming "Black" but now with multiple designations. The reproduction of these social hierarchies based on birthplace, skin color, ethnicity, and labor status—to name only a few—is crucial to understanding modern Brazil; first, they established the modern foundations of racial formation; second, they established the grammar for a very complex racial classification system; third, race formation and the racial classification system would lead to many of the current racial categories used in Brazil today; fourth, these categories would be used as the basis of social division as well as forms of social mobilization. These systems of racial classification will be dealt with throughout the book.

The Malês Revolt (Revolta dos Malês) of 1835 and the Abolition of Slavery

While slave revolts were common in Brazil and throughout the hemisphere, Salvador was the scene of one of the most effective and important slave rebellions in the Americas, commonly referred to as the Revolta dos Malês. According to the seminal work of João José Reis, a well-known and respected historian from Salvador, this 1835 revolt was led mainly by Muslim (Yoruba and Hausa) slaves. Though unsuccessful in winning freedom for the rebels, it had deep national repercussions. Slave rebellions both rural and urban in the nineteenth century were becoming more frequent in Bahia. Between 1820 and 1840, the province of Bahia witnessed a series of massive social revolts and wars by free and enslaved peoples alike. There was the anticolonial war, military revolts, anti-Portuguese manifestations, massive street riots, and of course a series of urban and rural slave rebellions. Bahia after independence from the Portuguese also experienced economic decline, droughts, unemployment, and inflation.

In the first three decades of the nineteenth century Salvador and its surrounding areas were rocked by a number of well-planned and organized social uprisings, and the Malês and Nagô were implicated. The word "Malês" is derived from *iamle*, the Yoruba word for Muslim. During this period slave rebellions both rural and urban in the nineteenth century were becoming more frequent in Bahia. The Muslim-led revolt that occurred in 1835 evolved from this long trajectory of revolts, and it is against this backdrop that the Malês revolt of 1835 occurred (Reis

1993, 21). Slaves in Salvador usually timed their uprisings to coincide with major events, like festival and holidays. According to the scholarly records, most of the participants and organizers came from the specific "nations" of Nagô or Malê. From roughly 1807 to the 1830s, slave uprisings reflected the development of collective ethnic identity across rural-urban boundaries among African-born male slaves who worked in groups. Preceding the 1835 revolt there was the insurrection of August 25, 1826, led by a Nagô slave who declared himself king in the tobacco-producing province of Recôncavo. In Cachoeria (a small town on the outskirts of Salvador) in April of 1827, slaves of the Engenho da Victoria and those from nearby plantations rebelled; and there was also the March 1828 revolt, when slaves united and fled from Salvador into the bush of Pirajá to join those from *engenhos* (sugar plantations) in Cabrito and Cabula.

The Revolta dos Malês in 1835 was perhaps the greatest spectacle of all modern slave revolts, standing out among the rebellions of the nineteenth century in Salvador. On January 24, 1835, a group of African-born slaves occupied the streets of Salvador for several hours as they confronted soldiers and armed civilians. The main organizers were identified as Malês and the primary goal of the revolt was to seize power of the local government. There were no indiscriminate attacks against citizens or random destruction of property, as their targets were strategic: they mainly attacked military barracks, police stations, and the local city headquarters. While the revolt lasted for only a few short hours, it is estimated that in its aftermath five hundred slaves were sentenced to death, sent to prison, whipped, or deported (Reis 2003, 73).

Along with sending shock waves across Brazil, the Revolta dos Malês ignited a hot debate on slavery and the slave trade in Brazil. The revolt included few if any Brazilian-born slaves. The lack of Brazilian-born Blacks was not unusual as native-born Blacks and mulatos did not take part in any of the more than twenty Bahian slave revolts prior to 1835. Afro-Brazilians' failure to act in the Revolta dos Malês can be explained by their tensions with Africans, which derived from their position within the political economy of Bahia's slave structure. The structure of the slave hierarchy cleverly reinforced and magnified differences: African-born slaves and Brazilian-born slaves as groups possessed different identities, languages, religions, and customs. Culturally the native-born Black was caught between being a "Westerner" and being African. Moreover, Afro-Brazilians had been born and raised in slavery, thus normalizing their status within a complex hierarchical system.

African-born slaves, unlike Brazilian-born slaves, were born free, in their homelands. Strangely, African-born slaves were constructed as the cultural "other" in larger society's view due to their continuing use of their native languages, with relatively limited acquisition of Portuguese, as well as their distinctively exotic cultural behavior, which was perceived as dangerous to the social order (Nishida 2003, 76). Both Afro-Brazilian slaves and Africans were enslaved, but they faced a different set of contradictions. While they were both locked into a rigid slave-based system, their strategic positions within this hierarchy produced different forms of consciousness. These differences became blurred once the majority of Blacks were Brazilian-born and after slavery was abolished.

After the Revolta dos Malês, in Salvador alone, there were an estimated two hundred hearings on the revolt and its consequences. The African and Black population were subjected to repression and brutality as well as a series of new restrictions that required them to register where they lived, obey a curfew, and pay a head tax (Harding 2000, 5). To this day the Revolta dos Malês remains part of the popular folklore and history of Salvador and everyone is familiar with this uprising. This revolt, however, did little to hasten the demise of slavery, and its wheels slowly ground on for another fifty-three years before it was finally abolished in 1888. The 1817 ban on trafficking slaves across the Atlantic was one of many prohibitions that signaled that the slave trade and slavery were slowly winding down. In formal political terms, Brazilian slavery was brought to an end by parliamentary legislation. By the 1840s there were other significant structural transformations occurring in Salvador's slave economy as urban slavery was in decline. The transition can be understood as the passing from a slave society to a slave-owning society, as Finley (1968) puts it. A slave society is a system wherein the political-economic elite are mainly dependent on slave labor as the basic mode of production. In contrast, a slave-own-ing society is one in which slavery exists but is not the main mode of production. By the middle of the 1840s, Salvador had become a slave-owning society.

The Abolition of Slavery in Brazil

The abolition of slavery in Brazil occurred in five major stages: the illegalization of the slave trade in Brazil in 1831; the effective prohibi-tion of the African slave trade in 1851; the passage of the Rio Branco Law in 1871, which freed children born to slave mothers and the 1885 law, which freed sexagenarians; and of course the Golden Law of 1888, which officially ended slavery. The first and second stages virtually ter-minated the transatlantic recruitment of slaves. The second deprived the slave system of its means of endogenous reproduction. The third and fourth accelerated legislative abolition of chattel slavery (Scott et al. 1988). While slavery was officially abolished in May of 1888, this official abolition did not free many slaves. Brazil's slave population, which had been as high as 50 percent of the national population, had dwindled to about 5 percent by the time of abolition (Conrad 1972). Ironically, Brazil would be the last Christian country to abolish slavery and the first to declare itself a racial democracy—that is, a country in theory bereft of both serious racial tension and racialized inequality (Andrews 1988).

The slow demise of slavery in the nineteenth century radically changed Bahia's social structures by creating a class of free people of color who stood outside the bounds of the formal relationship between slave and master. The end of slavery in some ways disarmed Bahia's slave-owning class, who became unable to control or regulate the lives of Afro-Bahians. Laws that had formerly restricted the activities of African-born slaves lost their power once the majority of Blacks were Brazilian-born. Absent the formal designation of a separate legal status for Afro-Brazilians, the laws in theory would now apply to all Brazil-ians. Abolition set in motion a profound social, cultural, and moral conflict in Bahia. Free people of color posed on many levels a serious threat to the formerly slavery-based ruling elite. They would have to devise new social codes and laws to control newly freed Afro-Bahians.

With the formal end of Brazilian slavery, Afro-Brazilians would face a new trajectory of uneven social forces. Unlike in the United States in 1865 and after the Civil War, there were no Thirteenth, Fourteenth, or Fifteenth Amendments; there would be no Freedmen's Bureau (an agency established to help ex-slaves transition to free status), nor any colleges and agricultural institutions established to help the newly freed slaves. As the historian George Reid Andrews argues, "Slavery was a traumatic experience for any society that experienced it, but when it was abolished it was replaced by new social, political, and economic arrangements that transformed the racial hierarchy while simultaneously preserving it" (Andrews 1988, 492). This was indeed the case for Brazil. Emancipation opened up a whole new set of questions for Brazilian society: it forced the ex-slaves, ex–slave owners, Blacks, mulatos, and whites to seriously deal with the position of Afro-Brazilians in the post-abolition period. In 1891, a new constitution was written, and by the turn of the century Brazil was struggling to establish a new social identity and to distance itself from its horrid slave past by transforming the nation into a modern republic. A key question after several centuries of slavery was what role Blacks would play in modern Brazil and how the arrival of thousands of white European immigrants would challenge or undermine Black mobility and social identity.

Afro-Bahians, in an effort to find a new footing and place in Brazilian society, sought to use culture as a form of agency in their effort to rebuild their lives. With the demise of slavery, the arrival of white immigrants mainly from Europe, and the rise of "race science," Afro-Brazilians now had to negotiate a powerful set of rough crosscurrents and new contradictions. In particular, race (pseudo) science sparked anxiety about Brazil's very large Black population and its high level of mestiçagem (racial mixture). At the same time, the forces of modernization sparked massive European immigration (mostly to southern Brazil) during the First Republic, from 1889 to 1930, which was premised on pushing aside former slaves in favor of whites in the new economy of the twentieth century. Bahia for the most part, however, lost out on the European whitening, as its economy was too poor and simply did not have the funds or the dynamism to attract the new arrivals. At this moment a new social order was emerging. The main question was, how would this new order impact Afro-Brazilians? How would it transform or undermine their identities and culture in the newly emerging Brazil? This is one of the main questions of the book: it will investigate the strategies and tactics employed by Afro-Brazilians in becoming full citizens. It is argued that issues of land rights (both rural and urban), identity, religion, and the rise of Black social movements are central to understanding social citizenship.

The Contradictions of Cultural Politics in Salvador da Bahia

1970s to the Present

This chapter focuses on Afro–social movements and the rise of civil society in Brazil from the middle of the 1970s until the present. It an- alyzes the burgeoning rise of blocos afros (carnival blocks or clubs) as horizontal Black social movements as they burst onto the scene in Brazil and Salvador in the 1970s and 1980s. Many of these movements were deemed "cultural" as they emphasized Afro-Diasporic music, religion, identity, and Black consciousness. At the same time similar, more politicized Black movements arose in Rio de Janeiro, São Paulo, and Salvador with explicit discourse framed around questions of racial equality, social discrimination, and citizenship. These various forma- tions—that is, blocos afros, Black social movements, and rising Black electoral political movements—have their early foundations in the emergence of Brazilian civil society during the transition to democ- racy in the mid- to late 1980s. Afro–civil society groups were central not only in expanding concepts of citizenship but also in developing new means of participation that were more horizontal than vertical in nature.

It is argued that Afro–civil society in Brazil and more specifically in Salvador emerged as a specific response to a broad set of complex issues and conditions deeply embedded in Brazil's unequal vertical social relations, political institutions, and cultural formations. These issues include the harsh and unequal administration of justice (police, jail, and prison); educational inequalities; the lack of access to the university system; stark discrimination in the political economy and labor market; negative, one-dimensional, and highly racialized images in the media; and a political culture and legal system devoid of any real or deep understanding of the unique status of Blacks as racialized second-class citizens (Goldstein 2003; Beato 2004).

Afro-cultural social movements in Brazil, while difficult to label, do mirror the horizontal nature of new social movements common across the Americas. Afro-Brazilian social movements emerged from below and of course outside the frame of traditional political institutions; they were not part of traditional political parties. Specifically, since Brazil was under a military dictatorship when many of these movements arose, they were of necessity horizontal. As horizontal movements in the post-dictatorship period they had to fight for space within the new democratic institutions as well as within emerging civil society institutions. In what Hardt and Negri (2001) call "constituent power," Afro-Brazilians had to not only shape and challenge outdated notions of Brazilian identity but also fight for social space within the newly emerging democratic structures simultaneously. Therefore, these movements are referred to as horizontal, as they had to do the following:

- Challenge and interrupt hegemonic notions of Brazilian identity as mainly white, male, and Christian;
- Challenge vertical political structures that excluded or marginalized Blacks while simultaneously creating new forms of participation from below;
- Challenge, critique, and transform racialized categories that had been deracialized over the centuries;
- Challenge and overturn the notion of racial democracy;
- Reposition the states' and civil society's views on racial inequality and force the state to recognize that it (racial inequality) is a legitimate political and social issue;

- Challenge and fight within leftist formations, parties, and movements regarding issues of racial discrimination;
- Create space within newly emerging civil society structures to challenge white vertical hegemony in order to allow for more open and thorough discussions of racial exploitation.

During the military dictatorship from 1964 to 1985 open discussions on key issues and grassroots mobilization were censured and denounced as subversive. Even some of the opposition groups could be characterized by authoritarian decision-making and vertical structures. However, the reconstitution of formal democracy following military rule from 1964 to 1985, and the emergence of Afro-Brazilian social movements during the final years of the dictatorship, propelled a series of burning questions into Brazilian national discourse. Opposition to military rule peaked in the early 1970s, and by the end of the decade, the country had begun a process of liberalization that enabled a large cross-section of diverse groups to challenge political and economic inequality through social movement and political mobilization. During the transition from military to civilian rule, Brazilian social movement groups sought to connect their struggle for democracy with their struggle for social justice (Andrews 1996, 483). Issues of racial equality, as well as of gender, emerged as important rallying cries for these new movements.

Afro-Brazilians across the country joined labor leaders and church officials, as well as the rural and urban poor, and began an unprecedented dialogue on the role of race and gender and how they structured opportunities and rewards in Brazilian society (Lovell 2000, 85). According to historian Paulina Alberto, during this time in Rio de Janeiro, Salvador da Bahia, and São Paulo, new Black political and cultural organizations emerged, drawing inspiration from the following: first, Afro-Portuguese decolonization movements in Africa (Alberto 2011, 246); second, international left movements; and third, the Afro–North American U.S. human rights movement. Black leaders, Afro–civil society, and key thinkers criticized the dictatorship and dominant racial ideologies (racial democracy) and also denounced racism while mobilizing Brazilians of color around strong Afro-referenced identities in order to reveal Brazil as a majority-Black nation (Alberto 2011).

Starting in the 1970s, Black movement groups, labor leaders, church officials, political exiles, and the international media put an unprecedented amount of pressure on the Brazilian military dictatorship to release the hundreds of political prisoners held and to end widespread torture. And during this time there was a call by these groups for an immediate transition to democracy (Green 2010). In fact these new social movements reengineered civil society, expressing democratic aspirations and broadening the experience of citizenship. Afro-Brazilians, as well as other key social actors, were central to these new democratic impulses.

The burgeoning Black movements of this era represented a break with previous levels of Black grassroots mobilization in Brazil as the scale of organization and the reach of these new movements grew as they expanded and gathered steam across the country. This chapter as well as chapter 4 examines the rise of these social movements as well as many issues and debates they tackled during this time.

In their important edited volumes, Dellacioppa and Weber (2012), Alvarez, Dagnino, and Escobar (1998), and Hendrik Kraay (1998) provide important theoretical markers for understanding exactly what is meant by cultural politics and its relation to Latin American social movements. Dagnino posits that cultural politics is important both for assessing the scope of the struggles of social movements and for the broader democratization of society and for highlighting the less visible and tangible implications of certain struggles (Alvarez, Dagnino, and Escobar 1998, 7). Cultural contestations are not simply by-products of political struggles but are also constitutive of social movements to redefine the meanings and inherent limitations of the political system (Alvarez, Dagnino, and Escobar 1998, 7). Cultural politics therefore is seen as both enactive and relational and refers to processes enacted when sets of social actors shaped by and embodying different cultural meanings and practices come into conflict with each other. Conceptually, this suggests that meanings and practices—particularly those theorized as marginal, oppositional, minority, residential, emergent, alternative, dissident, or some combination thereof—are all conceived in relation to the dominant cultural order. Culture is therefore by definition political because such meanings are constitutive of processes that implicitly or explicitly seek to redefine social relations of power (Alvarez, Dagnino, and Escobar 1998, 7). Thus, when movements deploy alternative conceptions of womanhood, nature, race, economics, politics, democracy, or citizenship that unsettle the dominant institutional setting and challenge the language of the hegemonic structure they are enacting cultural politics.

Along these lines, Kraay's volume, which focuses exclusively on Afro–cultural politics in Salvador and Bahia, systematically explores the intersection of Bahia's rich cultural history and politics by placing them within a historical time frame. By examining the broad intersection of culture, politics, history, racial discrimination, and social movements the volume makes an important contribution to understanding the centrality of Black cultural politics to Bahia and Brazil. It is argued that Afro-Bahian political history must be understood as an attempt to forge strong identities and maintain Black cultural formations in a hostile environment (Kraay 1998, 3). African-based identities, cultural formations, and social movements are said to be central to understanding modern Black politics in Brazil and Bahia.

Cultural politics, therefore, is at the center of Afro-Brazilian social movements and aesthetics, and in order to best understand blocos afros and cultural politics in Salvador it is necessary to trace the rise of the blocos as social movements starting in the 1970s as a unique cultural and political force. There has been a steady stream of rich literature and critical insights on the rise, significance, and relevance of blocos afros and carnival in Salvador, and much of the writing underscores five key areas: first, the founding of and the conditions paving the way for the rise of blocos and their re-Africanization of carnival in the 1970s; second, their performative and identity aesthetics as cultural signifiers; third, their role in articulating new forms of cultural politics and how such processes created new social spaces; fourth, the racialized Black body (both male and female) as a site of resistance, folklorization, and cooptation; and fifth, the process of commodification and commercialization (Riséro 1981; Stam 1988; Dunn 1992; Sansone 1995;

Agier 1995; Butler 2000; Altino de Souza 2006; Pinho 2010; Conceição 2010; Sterling 2012). These five areas provide a critical lens to understand the evolution and role of modern-day blocos in Salvador. Placing the blocos within a social movement frame presents a new layer of understanding of their evolution and early contribution to grassroots activism as well as insights into emergent cultural politics unfolding in Salvador from the 1970s to the present.

Afro-Bahian Cultural Productions

Afro-Bahian cultural productions are deeply anchored in the religion, music, and diverse cultural practices of West African peoples who were transported to Bahia as slaves to toil on sugar and tobacco plantations. The roots of the modern blocos stem from the *afoxés*, or African clubs, that were popular among Afro-Bahians at the start of the twentieth century (Dunn 1992, 13). Toward the end of the 1890s, these African clubs as cultural institutions proliferated across Salvador; however, elite white public opinion soon turned against them. Afro-Bahian cultural practices and rituals were considered below European civilization and came under serious attack. In particular, Candomblé and capoeira were routinely savaged and demonized in the Bahian press; Candomblé was seen as black magic, barbaric, and a haven for unhygienic conditions, and its medicinal customs were judged to be unsafe and even life-threatening. Capoeira was seen as a threat to peace and to the social order. Both Candomblé and capoeira suffered periodic campaigns of police repression and persecution, a persecution that was formalized with the rewriting of the penal code in 1890 (Ickes 2013, 4). By 1905 African-themed clubs were banned (Butler 2000, 177).

Between 1905 and 1914, African clubs in Bahia were banned from participating in carnival, as the spectacle of the "Black body" masquerading in drag as "African" was way too much for the dominant white elite of Salvador. As a result, many of these clubs faced repression as the white social elite of Bahia preferred a more sanitized, skim milk, Euro image of carnival. However, in 1949, under the name Filhos de Gandhi (sons of Gandhi) these clubs reappeared. Inspired by the anticolonial struggles of Mahatma Gandhi, and formed by Black and mulato dock

workers, they used the rhythms and symbols of West African traditions to articulate sounds of freedom in their music. These percussion
groups, made up mostly of men, were often members of Catholic societies or Candomblé houses and played traditional rhythms and songs
associated with the orixás.

The modern-day blocos are contemporary versions of the first African clubs from the turn of the century, and they burst onto the scene in
the 1970s. As cultural phenomena of the 1970s, blocos were influenced
by Black Rio, a cultural movement that flourished in Rio de Janeiro and
later spread to other parts of urban Brazil (Alberto 2009). Black Rio, or
the Black Soul Movement, was in turn influenced by North American
soul music and the U.S. Black power movement. Theoretically, while
the soul movement had no means to organize politically, it served to
unite Afro-Brazilians from different class backgrounds and was a powerful cultural force. Black Rio served as an important marker of identity and was a catalyst for identity-based politics that were emerging in
Brazil at this time (Turner 1985, 79).

In the 1970s many Afro-Brazilians, like Afro–North Americans,
sported large, bushy Afros, wore platform shoes (*estilo bleque pau*,
or Black power–style), and hosted large dance parties with DJs blast-
ing James Brown and other soul music from the United States. Black
Soul, like other Afro-Brazilian cultural expressions, was attacked as a
"movement with a racist philosophy" by the then municipal secretary
of tourism in Rio (Hanchard 1994, 114). Such a view was perhaps a
pretext for the anxiety of the white elite, both civil and military, that
the Black Soul Movement was a harbinger of a political protest movement by Afro-Brazilians (Hanchard 1994, 115). In part Black Soul was
a reaction to traditional samba schools where Blacks at times were
excluded as well as an expression of resentment of the fact that many
of the samba schools were dominated by middle- and upper-class
whites. The Black Rio movement as a corollary to the U.S. soul and
Black power movements neatly illustrates how the circuits of transnational Afro-Diasporic cultures and consciousness circulate and are ap-
propriated by peoples of African descent from one context to the next.
Black soul in Brazil was based on U.S. soul, and both were rooted in
Afro-Diasporic symbols and messages reaffirming Black music, dance,
and identity.

As the Rio soul movement slowly wound down the blocos afros began to emerge as a dynamic revolutionary new form of music and dance that changed the metrics of carnival and the tonality of Black social consciousness. It was within this context that the movement to re-Africanize Bahia's carnival was born and gained steam starting in the middle of the 1970s. And equally important, the arrival of the blocos must be seen within a century-long time frame and historical trajectory that began with African clubs being banned at the turn of the century in Salvador. In other words, African clubs, carnivals, brotherhoods, and sisterhoods are part of the Black cultural nucleus of Bahia, and despite attempts at social erasure, banning, or hegemonic suppression (police attack and negative media attention), they have not been able to socially "cleanse" Afro–cultural formations.

Ilê Aiyê and Olodum and the Rise of Black Cultural Politics in Salvador: The First Modern Blocos, 1970s to the Present

In the 1970s the new cultural formations of Black activist organizations arose in Salvador. These were blocos afros, or Black carnival groups that blended performances of African cultural themes with a sharp emphasis on antiracism, Black unity, and pride. Like the rise of activist student groups in Rio, the rise of the blocos in Bahia reflected the major shifts in Bahia society during the dictatorship's so-called "economic miracle."

By the middle of the 1970s, Salvador boomed with high-rise apartment buildings, shopping malls, and new industrial infrastructural projects like hydroelectric plants that were built outside of the city (Alberto 2011, 283). This new economic activity brought Bahia and Salvador more firmly into international consumer and media networks. At this time many working- and middle-class Blacks became increasingly likely to identify with Afro–solidarity messages from within Brazil and abroad. Many Black youths and activists became interested in and identified with African revolutionary struggles and the Black U.S. human rights movement. At the same time in Bahia, like the Black Soul movement in Rio, Bahia developed its own local soul and funk craze known as Black Bahia. Soul and funk music became increasingly popular and gave rise to a range of local musical styles identified with racial consciousness, including new carnival groups engaged in a new form of radical Black politics (Alberto 2011, 285). It is within this context that one of the first blocos, Ilê Aiyê, emerged and a new era of Black social mobilization and consciousness was unleashed.

In 1974, Antonio Carlos dos Santos (current president of Ilê Aiyê, and better known as Vovô) decided to create a carnival group that would focus on African-based themes and have a membership composed exclusively of dark-skinned Brazilians who had strong Afro-referenced identities (Alberto 2011, 284). It began as a movement of young people known as Zorra, who were from the neighborhood of Liberdade (Liberty), a predominant Black community in Salvador. On November 1, 1974, a member from Zorra founded Ilê Aiyê with the idea of honoring and affirming Black identity. Roughly a year later, in November 1975, Ilê Aiyê paraded the streets of Salvador as an official bloco dressed in colorful African garb and playing African-influenced rhythms. This was important for several reasons: first, it constituted the re-Africanization of carnival; second, Blacks previously excluded from carnival now had an all-Black bloco; and third, Ilê Aiyê, with this new bold act, ushered in a new period of Black social justice activism and consciousness in Salvador (de Almeida 2003, 49). Equally important as a new grassroots movement from below and from the margins, Ilê Aiyê offered bold new forms of participation in the cultural arena for Blacks locked out of Salvador's highly discriminatory social structures.

The founding of Ilê Aiyê as one of the first blocos in 1974, and the re-Africanization of carnival in 1975, set the stage for a new era of Black consciousness and social justice activism, and it served simultaneously as a platform for the newly emerging Black power movement in Salvador. At this unique historical juncture Brazil was still ruled by a military dictatorship, but political liberalization was slowly unfolding and civil society groups were becoming more and more common. Afro–carnival groups like Ilê Aiyê were the vanguard of an emerging radical platform to project a new form of Black identity and social consciousness. A radical new social landscape arose that altered traditional carnival practices by actualizing a specific Black performative aesthetic centering the Black body as a key point of reference while using music, dance, polyrhythmic structures, and Afro-Diasporic symbols rooted in African-inspired traditions. This was a revolutionary cultural shift given that Brazilians still lived under military dictatorship and Blacks had historically been excluded from carnival. Ilê Aiyê and the blocos that followed established a new framework for modern Afro-referenced identities based on reconstructing the past through the use of provocative body aesthetics, music, and dance.

Vovô, one of the founding members and current president, argues that Ilê Aiyê was breaking new ground by engaging in a new form of Black cultural politics because it was reaching out to thousands of Black people by helping them to positively reaffirm their cultural and social identities as Black Brazilians. In fact, Ilê Aiyê, by creating a Black bloco, was "political" according to Vovô: "We do the political with the cultural" (Alberti and Pereira 2007). As the first modern bloco, Ilê Aiyê is central to contemporary Afro-Bahian culture, modern Black consciousness, and Black social identity, as it is considered the guardian of African traditions, the "most beautiful of all," the most African bloco, and, of course, the oldest (Pinho 2010, 79). While blocos were opening new cultural spaces, they were simultaneously providing a direct challenge and critique of Brazil's discriminatory racial classification system (based on the early slave system of classification), in which Blacks were classified as pardo (Black), prêto (brown), or mulato (light-skinned).

In this system, dark-skinned Blacks were placed at the very bottom and white as well as light skin was idealized and worshipped. In the early days, Ilê Aiyê, in a direct repudiation of this racial classification system, restricted its membership to include only dark-skinned Afro-Brazilians. In other words, Ilê Aiyê reinvigorated and rescued the idea of "dark-skin Blackness" while reaffirming Africanness and, by definition, Pan-African and Black identity, concepts that had been distorted in Brazilian racial discourse. Ilê Aiyê thus set the tone and reflected a rising new Black social consciousness flowering in Brazil and Salvador. Ilê Aiye was not only the first bloco to re-Africanize carnival; it was also one of the first to simultaneously mobilize Blacks and denounce racial discrimination during the years of military dictatorship, when such activities were strictly prohibited. Ilê Aiyê was in fact engaged in

FIGURE 3.1. João Jorge Rodrigues, founding member and current president of the bloco Olodum. July 2013. Photo by author.

early radical cultural politics and acts of resistance that had deep political and social overtones. Soon thereafter other blocos would follow in their footpath.

Five years later, on April 25, 1979, Olodum was founded by sex workers, homosexuals, drug users, bohemians, and lawyers. It started out as a grassroots resistance organization in the historic neighborhood of Pelourinho and was created to fight extreme marginalization, racial inequality, and widespread social discrimination (Rodrigues 1999, 47). João Rodrigues, the current president, argues that Olodum was born to defend and articulate Black culture and that the defense of Black culture is "political" in Salvador and Brazil (Rodrigues 1999, 47). Olodum is currently the most famous bloco in Brazil. Building on the success of Ilê Aiyê, they were catapulted to success and became famous for their pulsating drumming sessions held on Tuesday nights in Pelourinho, when it was then a run-down, drug-infested neighborhood.

In contrast to Ilê Aiyê, Olodum early on decided to admit whites and mestizos as members and made a conscious decision to involve themselves in the political struggles of Salvador in the 1980s. It has carefully cultivated its image as a culturally diverse bloco that reaffirms Black identity within a broad multicultural framework. It was Olodum's commercial collaborations, first with Paul Simon on his 1990s album *Rhythm of the Saints* and later with Michael Jackson in his now-famous video "They Don't Care about Us" (1996), that firmly established their international credentials and made them the best-known bloco. They have also collaborated with Jimmy Cliff, Ziggy Marley, and other reggae singers from the Caribbean. Other blocos of course—like Muzenza, Ara Ketu, Puxada Axé, Malês, and Debalês—would soon follow as many sprang up in neighborhoods across Salvador.

Olodum's rehearsals and drumming sessions soon became famous and foci for local activists, poets, musicians, and tourists from all over the world. Its legendary Tuesday night rehearsals reinvented the tradition of benediction, a six o'clock evening mass, at the Church of Rosário in Pelourinho, which became a common gathering point for Afro-Bahian youths (Butler 1998, 170). Their music, much like that of Ilê Aiyê, fuses social commentary and cultural politics with fragments of Afro-Brazilian history and links them to a transnational Black identity. Their Tuesday night rehearsals, along with the powerful percussion and the wail of music, became their signature trademark.

Along with having the ability to mobilize their constituencies, the blocos were able to deliver powerful messages to Salvador's dispossessed urban poor masses. Issues of Black identity rooted in a Pan-African frame included the lethal hand of the law and police brutality, social cleansing by death squads, lack of respect and dignity, and unemployment—to name only a few—and such themes were articulated with airtight clarity by the blocos, resonating deeply with the poor Black youth scattered across the urban favelas in Salvador. The blocos were in fact creating a radical new social grammar and constructing new ways of communicating the language of marginality, underscoring how Brazil's highly unequal social system had kept Blacks permanently peripheral and locked out. It was within this social context that the blocos were born as militant Black organizations to denounce racial discrimination as well as reaffirm Black identity and personhood.

As blocos and cultural movements they were uncovering new terrain and operating from a radical new cultural angle as well as opening new social spaces to talk about and critique racialized oppression and class inequality. On the transnational level, according to João Rodrigues, the early blocos like Ilê Aiyê and Olodum were deeply influenced by the national liberation movements of the Afro-Portuguese countries of Mozambique, Guinea Bissau, and Angola in the 1970s as African books and literature written in Portuguese circulated widely in Salvador. In particular, the ideas of Amilcar Cabral of the African Party for the Independence of Guinea-Bissau and Cape Verde (PAIGC), Samora Michel of the Mozambique Liberation Front (FRELIMO), and Agostinho Neto of the Popular Movement for the Liberation of Angola (MPLA) influenced their views of culture, identity, and struggle.

Blocos arose, therefore, as a direct reaction and challenge to very specific social and political conditions that kept Blacks outside the official channels of public discourse. Historically Blacks in Salvador and across Brazil have had limited options for effecting change through established political networks and the traditional bureaucratic order. Afro-Bahians, through blocos and other cultural productions, have established alternative institutions that have accorded them some degree of political leverage (Butler 1998, 158). According to Butler, the creation and construction of new power bases through Afro-Bahian cultural institutions in the late twentieth and early twenty-first centuries must be seen as an attempt by Afro-Bahians to create alternative structures to correct and counteract centuries of political and cultural exclusion and social devaluation. Since the 1970s, the blocos in Salvador have grown in power, number, and prestige, and through their social and cultural activities they have been very effective in recruiting and maintaining a hard core and dedicated cadre of supporters, mostly from the ranks of Salvador's urban poor and middle classes. Currently in Salvador the blocos are the main venues for the creation of strong Afro-referenced identities and Black cultural symbols. Many blocos, along with having strong followings in Brazil, are also well known and followed internationally. In Salvador, Ilê Aiyê is commonly described as the first and most "African" bloco whereas Olodum is called the most famous.

According to Patricia Pinho, a scholar who writes extensively on the blocos, they arose out of the need to connect tradition to modernity, a need that incorporates the acceptance of cultural elements from different areas of the Black Diaspora (Pinho 2010, 80). Moreover, the Black ethnic identity that blocos reinvented not only corresponded to local forms of racism and racial exclusion but also connected to transnational consciousness-raising movements among the Black Diaspora (Pinho 2010, 79). Blocos challenged the prevailing hegemonic racial discourse that claimed Brazil was somehow free of racial discrimination despite its long past of slavery and therefore made a significant contribution to the growth of antiracist organizing starting in the middle of the 1970s that continues into the present. Through the use of music, songs, dance, and, later, community programs, blocos were able to unmask and deconstruct racial oppression by openly denouncing racial discrimination against Blacks. The irony is that during this time (in the early days) the blocos were accused of racism because they were openly talking about racism, racial inequality, and racial discrimination, subjects considered impolitic by the prevailing hegemonic and everyday discourses embedded in a fantasy of Brazil as a racial paradise.

According to Walter Altino de Souza, an intellectual-activist and expert on the blocos from Salvador, the rise of the blocos reflected the two sides of a simmering-hot debate on the proper role and intersection of culture and politics in Afro-Brazilian social movement circles in the 1970s. Each side had a distinct view on the role of culture and politics as vehicles of grassroots mobilization. One wing, represented by the cultural groups, emphasized music, dance, and religion, and they did not consider themselves or their organizations as expressly political. On the other side were savvy political activists, who wanted more concrete action based on grassroots organizing, political education, and promoting Black consciousness. The genius of the blocos—on some level—is that they were able to synthesize these tensions as they addressed or at least spoke to this dilemma by creatively deploying Afro-Bahian cultural formations—that is, song, music, and dance—to address a whole range of complicated political and social issues. And, at the same time, they were able to disseminate a message that catered to and resonated widely with thousands of poor disenfranchised citizens in Salvador and across Brazil (Altino de Souza 2013).

Ilê Aiyê and Olodum as leading blocos do, however, have slightly different social and historical markers that distinguish them. On some level these differences are less important today, but they do serve as an important reference point to understand the blocos' histories and current work. Ilê Aiyê's working principle at its founding was an Afrocentric, Pan-Africanist worldview, and Africa was and still is a clear point of reference in their music and social philosophy. In the beginning it restricted its membership to only prêtos (dark-skinned Blacks), and the base of its membership for some time was Black middle-class intellectuals. Musically Ilê Aiyê uses mainly percussion-based instrumentation, and, as previously stated, its base of operation is in the community of Liberdade.

In contrast, Olodum was founded within a multicultural Pan-African orientation rooted loosely in a Marxist framework, and their membership base in the early days was the urban working class and underclass, or lumpenproletariat. Their membership has traditionally been open to all, thus its multicultural perspective. Musically Olodum is more apt to include reggae and Caribbean-inflected rhythms, incorporating guitars and some brass instruments in its work. It is better known internationally and has a larger worldwide following. According to Patricia Pinho, Ilê Aiyê has constructed itself as being concerned and focused on "Blackness" whereas Olodum is sometimes constructed as not having the depth or the authority to deal with "Africanness," while the latter is described as more original and as having not deviated from its African roots (Pinho 2010, 93). In other words, it is argued, Ilê Aiyê represents authentic "African Blackness" and Olodum does not. Within the context of Salvador these discourses have many levels of meaning and significance. For example, the community of Liberdade, where Ilê Aiyê operates and was founded, is universally considered "the hood," or a real Black neighborhood, whereas Pelourinho, despite being majority-Black and poor, is not considered "Black" in Salvador's racial discourse. Debates on Black or African authenticity—that is, who is "really" Black or who is "Blacker" than whom—are found in discourses not only in Brazil but throughout the African Diaspora. The competing discourses and counter-discourses between Ilê Aiyê and Olodum mirror some of the long-standing and deep discursive notions on the social wages of Blackness—for example, when Blacks determine who is "really" Black versus when non-Blacks determine who is Black.

Altino de Souza argues that modern blocos should be seen through three distinct lenses: first as sociocultural groups, second as educational organizations (NGOs), and third as businesses, meaning that they operate as separate entities from the NGOs and therefore follow laws established for businesses, or for-profit enterprises (Altino de Souza 2013). These three entities, while separate, also intersect and overlap in the various forms of their work. Altino de Souza believes they form three legs of the same stool and must be seen as complementary on one hand and contradictory on the other. Since the late 1980s, the blocos have expanded and developed community outreach strategies, including organizing educational schools and programs as well as pedagogical projects and businesses; and both have established what appear to be very successful businesses. Their cultural exchange programs include elementary school programs, after-school cultural programs, and pedagogical projects.

The Blocos and Black Education: Cultural Politics as a Political Project

In 1988, Ilê Aiyê founded Escola Máe Hilda (the Máe Hilda School), which is named after the mother of one of the principal founders. The school is located in Liberdade, the base of Ilê Aiyê's operation, and run by a board of twelve people, with Vovô at the top. Escola Máe Hilda offers classes to roughly one hundred students from first to third grade, and a majority of the students live in Liberdade. The teachers hail from many backgrounds; however, it is safe to say that many are practitioners of Candomblé whereas most of the students are Catholic and Protestant. The school is impressive in scope and size; the classrooms are bright, colorful, and airy, with plenty of space for the children to move about freely. All of the classrooms have pictures of well-known people of African descent prominently displayed. According to Vovô and one of the teachers, students study math, science, Portuguese, and history (that is, African, Afro-Brazilian, and Brazilian history), and all of the kids receive a meal and snack every day. The school is free, supported by the bloco's business ventures as well as Brazilian corporations like Petrobras, the Brazilian oil company.

Ilê Aiyê's Pedagogical Educational Project is another part of its work in Salvador. It was started in 1995 with the idea of incorporating African history and culture into the public school curriculum of Salvador. The project's pedagogical principle is "fostering the reclaiming of African culture and its influences on Brazil within the perspective of a pluri-cultural society through racial identity, the development of critical thinking, and self-esteem of Black children and adolescents" (Pinho 2010, 119). The project has ties with five public schools, including an elementary school and a public high school. The teachers, directors, and councilors in these schools participate in an annual six-week course on African history that is led and taught by Ilê Aiyê teachers. This project is linked to Ilê Aiyê's early philosophy and history, as in the 1980s it was one of the first groups that advocated for public schools to incorporate and teach African history. Ilê Aiyê's support and partnership with public schools is based on the following contentions: first, that Salvador's (and Brazil's) public schools provide poor-quality instruction; second, that public schools lack the funds, teacher training, and methodology necessary to implement high-quality instruction; third, that schools don't teach Afro-Brazilian and Black history. Ilê Aiyê therefore developed this project as a way to help some of the public schools offer classes on African and Afro-Brazilian history.

Olodum operates its own after-school program, Escola Critaiva Olodum (Olodum Creative School), located in Pelourinho, and like Ilê Aiyê, it serves to reaffirm Black identity and give students a cultural education for a few years. Each year the school receives about one thousand applications, and in order to be considered for admission applicants must first be enrolled in a public school. Students study arts, science, math, history, citizenship, and ethics. Olodum's project is an after-school program and is open to all the students from several of Salvador's communities and not just children from Pelourinho (de Jesus 2014). The main focuses of their after-school program are art, dance, music, and information technology. Olodum and Ilê Aiyê as well as other blocos share common goals and points of interest and believe these social, cultural, and pedagogical activities serve to enhance the living conditions of the Black population, and their educational outreach methodologies emphasize human rights and the interests of the Afro-Brazilian population. By creating alternative social institutions to serve the interest of Blacks in Salvador, blocos have created new forms of Black consciousness and provided education to thousands of Black schoolchildren and training to hundreds of teachers.

What Is the Price of Success? Commodification and Cooptation

Since their founding, blocos have created bold new forms of identity representation, served as a platform for political contestation and grassroots education and mobilization, established social justice activist networks and community outreach programs, established primary educational schools as well as musical and technical training programs, engaged in politics by supporting political candidates, and established lucrative small businesses. Currently Ilê Aiyê and Olodum both have established what appear to be very successful businesses and earn revenues through lucrative business and licensing deals. Over the last two decades these blocos have entered local politics and have endorsed and campaigned for politicians, negotiated deals, and accepted support from corporations as they have become for-profit businesses. Some blocos now charge for their concerts, performing in special shows, and sell music (CDs, DVDs) as well as T-shirts, caps, pants, coffee mugs, key chains, and an assortment of other goods. It is almost impossible to visit Salvador without seeing the merchandise of Olodum and Ilê Aiyê for sale in shops or on the streets. And their concerts both free and paid continue to draw large, enthusiastic crowds of loyal fans from across Salvador, Brazil, and the world. The key questions are, to what extent do such programs serve as a base for social and political empowerment? And do their small business enterprises and commercial ties compromise their social agenda of Black empowerment?

Michael Hanchard's book *Orpheus and Power* (1994) raised an important point regarding the construction of hegemonic power and the intersection of culture with respect to Afro-Brazilian cultural articulations. Building on Antonio Gramsci's notion of hegemony, Hanchard poses the following question: how do subordinate individuals/groups forge counter-hegemonic values out of existing, reactionary ones without reproducing the latter in new forms (Hanchard 1994, 20)? This fundamental question, according to Hanchard, is relevant to most power struggles on the national scale and is therefore key to understanding how Afro-Brazilians have attempted to create alternative political discourses regarding the reproduction of racial inequality and the creation of new forms of positive identities.

Blocos were born as Black militant organizations to challenge the dominant hegemonic patterns of racial inequality and promote positive Black identity as well as serve the interests of Salvador's urban masses. However, these newly established political relationships and business ventures raise a series of thorny and difficult questions: Has the power of the market and mainstream clientele politics diminished the emancipatory logic of the blocos' political activities? Does the "cultural marketing of Blackness" or the "folklorization" of Blackness devalue or undermine positive Black identity? To what extent have blocos been able to impact local politics by electing individuals to office who might implement a progressive democratic vision that serves the needs of the poor urban masses? Has the cultural power of the blocos and their business and political relationships led to a better material situation for Blacks in Salvador and Bahia? Simply put, have the blocos sold out? And if so, to whom?

In order to best understand the evolution of blocos it is important to narrate a series of events that unfolded in Salvador in the 1980s. Pelourinho—a historic neighborhood and Olodum's main site of operation—was declared a World Heritage Site by UNESCO in 1985. This official designation unleashed and set in motion a powerful set of crosscurrents and conflicting interests. At the time, Pelourinho was a dilapidated, run-down, and crime-infested neighborhood, but the new designations by UNESCO meant that if the area could be revitalized, lots of money could be made. At the start of the 1990s, supported by multinational lenders like the World Bank, the city began to spend millions of dollars on revitalization projects to restore historic buildings, churches, and plazas in Pelourinho. After years of delays and negotiations with local residents and community groups, the government implemented a program of restoration to refurbish many of these historic sites that were literally falling apart. In 1991, O Patrímonio Artístico e Cultural (the Institute of Artistic and Cultural Heritage), a state-funded operation, led a massive revitalization program to modernize Pelourinho. With a budget of almost forty million reales and led by the legendary governor of Bahia Antônio Carlos Magalhães (mayor 1967–1970, governor 1971–1975, 1979–1983, 1991–1994), the revitalization plan was controversial from day one.

Olodum, which had been involved in the revitalization plans and negotiations, now found itself caught in the treacherous crosscurrents of local grassroots advocacy (that is, support for poor Blacks, one of their key constituencies) on one side and powerful, state-led developmental interests on the other. Olodum, of course, shared the interest of the state, as it wanted a revitalized Pelourinho, but in order to achieve this, local residents would have to be expelled. Many of these residents thought that Olodum would be their advocate and not their adversary. Olodum's long-term interest—that is, to revitalize and rebuild Pelourinho into an important tourist site—directly conflicted with the interests of some of the longtime residents who were poor and Black and wanted to remain. As historian Anadelia Romo points out, as the city undertook plans for a massive and violent rezoning effort, the revitalization effort crystalized officials' simultaneous valorization of an Afro-Bahian culture while disregarding the conditions and lives of Afro-Bahians (Romo 2010, 153): what was termed "revitalization" for some was "social cleansing" for others. Many residents, mainly poor and Black people, were forcefully removed from their homes, some at gunpoint. It is estimated that roughly six hundred families were "relocated" and that the compensation for their removal was between US$400 and $800 per family (A Tarde 1992). Black inhabitants were evicted so that Black history could be turned into a commodity. Romo argues that while Afro-Bahians were valued as part of Bahia's past, living Afro-Bahians in Pelourinho proved an inconvenient obstacle to future development (Romo 2010, 153).

In this scenario, commercial "success" and "development" were translated into implementing a series of urban renewal projects that served only the residents who were allowed to stay (not all were removed) and the interests of local businesses. To their credit Olodum, before anyone thought the area was valuable, established Pelourinho as its base of operation and has been instrumental in its "revitalization." Olodum is currently a key player in the state-led investing in Pelourinho, which, as noted, often conflicts with the interests of at least some of the residents. The renovations that were desperately needed did benefit other blocos and some artists as well as retailers, hotels, and restaurants. The revitalization brought fancy restaurants, art galleries, and expensive shops, but many of the residents who currently live in Pelourinho cannot afford to shop or eat in these establishments. There exists a silent but sharp tension between the residents and some of the businesses, and these tensions, while not obvious on the surface, are slowly becoming apparent. The gentrification of Pelourinho is a symbol of Black experiences with mass displacement and the repressive regimes of urban restructuring (Pinho 2010). Currently Pelourinho is central to Salvador's and Bahia's images as the epicenter of Afro-Brazilian culture, and it serves as a global symbol and magnet for both Brazilian and foreign tourists. As one long-term resident of Pelourinho and active member of the Association of Friends and Residents of the Historic Center said, "It's now a shopping mall for rich tourists" (Pereira 2013).

Ilê Aiyê has received generous support from the giant construction firm Odebrecht and the Brazilian oil company Petrobras. In its early years, Ilê Aiyê chose not to play a role in electoral politics; however, over the last couple of decades it has entered the electoral fray by openly supporting candidates. The 2000 mayoral reelection campaign of Antônio Imbassahy received support from Ilê Aiyê; Carlinhos Brown, the famous singer and promoter of carnivals; and Gerônimo, a local singer and cultural hero. Brown's and Gerônimo's voices and images were used extensively throughout the campaign (Pinho 2010, 200). The ads used in the electoral campaign were based on carnival images from six months prior, meaning important Black cultural symbols were used to add muscle and deliver political campaign ads to Salvador's urban masses. The new relationship between the blocos, which emerged to challenge white hegemonic power, and Salvador's white ruling elite appears at least on the surface to directly contradict their earlier missions, as they were founded as autonomous agents of social change free from the influence of patronage and conservative political forces. It is difficult to see how such relationships confer or advance the broad interests of Salvador's urban poor.

Along with the blocos there are other Black cultural groups that have formed strategic alliances with local and state government officials as well as with business and tourist interests to "promote roots tourism" or the "cultural marketing" of Afro-Bahia (Pinho 2008). This cultural marketing includes tours to quilombo communities, spectating Candomblé ceremonies and capoeira performances, and of course watching performances by blocos. State forces, business interests, blocos, and Black cultural groups have entered into strategic relations and transformed Afro–cultural productions into a form of symbolic Black cultural capital. Some argue that in this process Black cultural capital becomes overly commodified, thereby losing its emancipatory logic and its counter-hegemonic positioning. Against this backdrop, questions arise: Is the cultural capital of Afro-Bahia being crassly exploited and thus working against Blacks? Or is it not being deployed properly?

Within the larger hegemonic matrix and despite attempts by the blocos and other groups to create positive images, a series of complicated distortions are at play. Blacks in Salvador are constructed via processes of commodification as "happy," "obedient," extremely musical, gifted singers, and exceptional athletes and are shaped into the image of the immaculate Black body—both male and female—which as a key site of contestation, cooptation, and exploitation is central to hegemonic positioning, from the capoeirista to the *acarajé* vendor (a Bahian woman dressed in white who sells African-inspired food). Across Salvador the Black body is always on full display, whether as the main site of the social production of performance like song, music, and dance; in the daily image of Blacks selling food on the streets; or on the beach as an object of hypersexual gratification for both men and women. In fact the wholesale commodification of the Black body and culture may have become an impediment to social power.

Gilroy argues that the super-affirmation of the Black body in the realm of culture as set of symbols creates a comfort zone that becomes more artificial as dissident culture becomes ever more spectacle-like and aestheticized. Thus, according to Gilroy, Black culture becomes "revolutionary conservative" since it is revolutionary in appearance but conservative in content (Gilroy 2000, 70). Pinho points out that as a consequence of commodification Bahian Afro–cultural production runs the risk of becoming an arena that allows little concrete resistance against a hegemonic system that reproduces racial dominance and race and class inequalities (Pinho 2010, 213). Against this backdrop, and retuning to Hanchard, how do subordinate individuals/groups forge counter-hegemonic values out of existing, reactionary ones without reproducing the latter in new forms?

Fernando Conceição, an intellectual and social justice activist from Salvador, argues that cultural commodification by the blocos and Black cultural producers has "repackaged" Blackness and distanced the culture from its revolutionary agency. The depth, texture, and political substance of Black identity and the urgency of critical issues have been severely undermined by market forces and through alliance with the traditional ruling elements of Bahia (2010). He believes that Black cultural capital, which was accumulated in centuries of struggle, is now being undermined by the same people who claim to defend it. The cultural power of Afro-Bahia and the formation of blocos, according to Conceição, have not led to a better material situation for most Blacks (Conceição 2010, 21). Along these lines, cultural commodification, according to Hanchard, freezes or hypostatizes cultural practices, divorcing them from the histories and attendant modes of consciousness that brought them into being, and limits the range of alternative articulations and movements available to Afro-Brazilian groups.

The marketing of Afro-Bahia is now part of official state discourse. The Brazilian state (local and regional), some Black cultural groups, the tourism-industrial complex, and some U.S. universities and colleges have entered into various alliances to package, market, sell, and present Afro-Bahian culture or "folklore" as uniquely Brazilian on one hand and African on the other—"milking mama Africa," in the words of Pinho. These processes, which are regional, national, and transnational, raise some important questions. According to Josélio Teles dos Santos, through careful hegemonic construction of "folklore," the state—now in conjunction with other actors—manipulated the symbolic realm of culture, first to gain political control and second to realize economic gains. State cultural initiatives therefore have serious political meaning; they did not simply recognize the existence of Afro-Brazilian cultural expressions and their contributions to Brazilian society. Rather, the state sought political control and what might be termed symbolic surplus value for economic development, in particular the reproduction of national and regional identity that could be marketed by Bahia's tourism-industrial complex (Teles dos Santos 1998, 123).

Currently in Salvador the blocos are still very active, and they have grown in size and prestige as they have become more and more able to project their power across Salvador, Brazil, and the globe. Their positive messages, rhetoric, and image represent the projection of strong Afro-referenced social identity and Black cultural capital. More importantly, the blocos and those who have followed them have built important social institutions like schools and after-school programs that have served thousands of poor students over the years. Given their central role in carnival, tourism, education, and community activism, they will continue to construct and form an integral part of Salvador's cultural and social identity. Carnival and blocos are now synonymous with each other and thus central to Salvador's, Bahia's, and Brazil's image and ever-expanding tourism industry.

However, the business ventures and new commercial ties call into question their ability to continue to challenge Salvador's ruling hierarchies. And while they continue to serve poor and often forgotten constituencies, their grassroots participatory structures have eroded and been replaced with top-down, vertical styles of operation. Both Ilê Aiyê and Olodum now operate corporate-style boards of directors and are run by personality-driven individuals wielding lots of power. In short, the power of the market, questionable political alliances, ties to megacorporations like Petrobras and Odebrecht, and their corporate style have severely compromised their autonomy as well as their organic grassroots credentials. The blocos in some ways are subordinate social groups competing with each other over the form, content, and legitimacy of Afro-Brazilian identity. And their carnival activities, concert performances, schools, and social programs are part of the larger contention for legitimacy and social entry into the broader sphere of Brazilian social relations (Green and Scher 2007, 11–12). As Patricia Pinho points outs, Ilê Aiyê's discursive practices point to authenticity and a deeper, more organic connection to Africa whereas Olodum is seen as manifesting a form of "integrational hybridity" of lesser purity (Sterling 2012). And unlike in the old days in the time of their founding, Ilê Aiyê and Olodum, while of course still connected to the Black masses and the middle classes, do not challenge or represent a threat to the social order because they now on some level represent a wing of state hegemonic discourse for Black identity. They are, however, still able to promote Afro-referenced identity and project themselves as grassroots entities.

The Emergence of the Movimento Negro Unificado

The Rise of a New Racial Politics

Alongside the rise of blocos and Black Rio in the 1970s and new forms of Afro-referenced identity there were hot debates unfolding about the relationship between Black culture and politics and about the proper role of Black culture as a form of political resistance and grassroots mobilization. This new racial politics advocated the articulation of "Black culture" as a strategy for mobilizing, politicizing, and raising the consciousness of the Black masses. In 1978 the Movimento Negro Unificado Contra Discriminação Racial (MNU) emerged on the scene at a time when many Black cultural groups and associations were seen or constructed as cultural (Black Rio and early blocos) because it was thought that many of these groups lacked explicit or clearly defined political strategies—that is, antiracist platforms and grassroots social action. In stark contrast, as a radical new formation MNU wanted a conscious political project that squarely addressed racial inequality in the broader frame of Brazilian politics and civil society. This bold articulation of a new racial politics attempted to unify Black movement groups grounded in the understanding that racism was a key political issue. At this time many cultural groups emphasized dance, music, and religion divorced from the social and political context; however, there was an urgent argument being articulated that Black culture, as a site of resistance, should be used as an instrument for raising and cultivating Black consciousness and for grassroots political mobilization.

Founded four years after Ilê Aiyê (1974) and one year before Olodum, MNU (1978) arose out of the dense fog of Brazilian politics of the late 1970s. As a radical new expression of civil society, its roots grew out of the nonpolitical realm and became linked to the state through their insertion into the fine webs of power as they reworked power's very knowledge, acting in capillary spaces of the state apparatus. MNU and other social movement groups thus gained a certain degree of power vis-à-vis the state (Gomes da Cunha 1998, 222). Lélia González, one of MNU's founding members and a brilliant theoretician, represented one of the key theorists of the intersection of culture and politics. González suggested that "politics" and "culture," if theorized separately, could not carry out the transformation project she was articulating. In other words dance parties, samba clubs, and the traditional political strategies of left-based political parties (mass meetings and radical politicization) were not effective in raising the consciousness of or mobilizing the Black masses. In González's view there had to be a careful synergy between the cultural and the political. According to González, and the others who shared her view, neither "culturalism" nor "traditional left politics" addressed the profound social contradictions that plagued Brazil's racialized social problems; it was argued that "culturalism" actually reinforced a benevolent image of Brazil as a homogenous population bereft of race, class, and gender fissures (Gomes da Cunha 1998, 223). The task for many Black activists therefore was to link Black culture to radical Black politics and social transformation.

Against the backdrop of these debates a series of events set the movement on fire. Among them, the torture and murder of Robson Silveira de Luz, a Black taxi driver, by the São Paulo police in April of 1978—one of the many injustices against Blacks—mobilized activists to take concrete action and served as a catalyst to new Black social mobilization and the formation of MNU. MNU was established by activists from São Paulo and Rio de Janeiro, and their first act of public defiance was to organize a demonstration in front of the municipal theater building in downtown São Paulo to protest the murder of Silveira de Luz and racial discrimination in Brazil (Hanchard 1994, 125). Police brutality and other state-sanctioned violence against Blacks led activists of São Paulo and Rio de Janeiro to organize a large-scale public act of resistance and defiance.

The organizers in São Paulo mobilized various pockets of the Black community and launched a grassroots campaign that encouraged as many people as possible to attend their planned public demonstration. Given that such public demonstrations were expressly prohibited by the military dictatorship many activists knew they were putting a lot on the line; however, the time to act had finally arrived. On July 7, 1978, two thousand people gathered on the steps of the São Paulo Municipal Theater and read an open letter that denounced racial discrimination, police violence, unemployment, and marginalization of Afro-Brazilians (Hanchard 1994, 125). This public demonstration and act of defiance opened a new chapter of Black radical social movement history in Brazil. The Movimento Negro Unificado Contra Discriminação Racial later shortened its name to MNU (Movimento Negro Unificado).

MNU, like the blocos, arose as a direct response to deep social inequalities and specific forms of social violence affecting Black populations across Brazil. It emerged at a unique historical juncture within the matrix of Brazilian politics. Several key factors explain its rise. The first was the intersection of new levels of Black consciousness and racial politics. The second was the rise of social movements and transnational advocacy groups across the political spectrum domestically and internationally. At this time there were Brazilian groups organizing in the United States and Europe against the dictatorship who were challenging the military regime's grip on power. The third was the impact of the U.S. Black power and African national liberation movements. And the fourth was that these conditions, along with the process of democratization unfolding, created new space for emerging civil society groups across Brazil. Urban Black groups of mainly university students, journalists, artists, religious groups, and professionals began to insert themselves in a variety of ways into the discussion of race relations in Brazil (Gomes da Cunha 1998, 222). These movements and debates began with a substantive critical analysis of one of the most glaring forms of oppression experienced by many Afro-Brazilians—that is, the violence perpetrated by state police institutions. The struggle against the military regime thus presented insurgent Black movement activists an opportunity within the larger struggle to advance a series of critiques of the treatment of Blacks by state institutions. The police, courts, jails, and prisons, it was argued, penalized more frequently and more harshly poor, brown, and Black people.

Race, class, and gender as key organizing principles, as well as a focus on state-sponsored violence against Black and brown people, emerged as some of MNU's key themes and critiques. Thus the calculus of race, class, and gender shaped how MNU and other Black groups understood social justice and political economy. Issues of social justice, employment, land, and education were now analyzed along this axis. Were race relations in Brazil coercive? And if so, how would MNU develop the language, strategies, and organizing platform to reach out to the Afro-Brazilian masses? Was the process of racialization in a deracialized society a political question? Who is Black? Should Blacks who commit everyday crimes be considered political prisoners? These questions constituted only a tiny fraction of the many complex issues that MNU and other groups had to squarely address. Additionally they faced the task of deconstructing centuries of racialized hegemonic structures, ideas, and thought processes that effectively positioned racial discrimination as a nonissue—including the idea that racial discrimination in Brazil did not exist. In addition to the murder of da Silva, MNU was also set into motion by a series of earlier discussions and debates launched by regional Black movement groups that believed there was an urgent need to form a single structure at the national level to coordinate, facilitate, and organize the larger antiracist struggle across Brazil.

The key architects of MNU envisioned an independent national-level organization that would synthesize and link the main issues of Black communities scattered across Brazil. As a newly emerging civil society organization with an explicitly antiracist platform its main aim was to cultivate strong Black consciousness and combat racial discrimination in all of its forms. Mirroring the power of leftist revolutionary ideas and the fervor of the Afro-Portuguese national liberation movements of the 1970s, MNU founders initially framed their struggle against racism as part of the larger hegemonic project to eradicate capitalism in Brazil. Their earlier statutes for example, elaborated by Yedo Ferreira and Amauri Pereira, two of MNU's early members, were based on the organizational framework of the Marxist Frente de Libertação de Moçambique (Mozambique Liberation Front), or FRELIMO (Alberto 2011, 292).

Toward the end of 1979, MNU had established its organizational and social identity by clearly defining the scope of its work, outlining its programmatic vision, and defining its working structure via a series of national assemblies and national congresses held across Brazil from 1978 to 1980. It first organized itself based on the model of communist cells, known as *centros de luta* (struggle centers), assigning small groups to spread out among Black communities, leading discussions about pressing issues and engaging in consciousness-raising. Central to its work was the attempt to make its presence known across Brazil, and it established centros de luta in Porto Alegre, Bahia, Belo Horizante, and other cities across Brazil. By 1979 it had a strong political orientation and an antiracist message, and it denounced sexism and homophobia. Moreover, it had a serious analysis and critique of the systematic nature of police violence aimed at Black people in Brazil. Additionally, it recognized the global character of racism and was committed to the struggle of all oppressed peoples and groups around the globe (Covin 2006, 85).

However, MNU's top-heavy Marxist emphasis in its early years alienated many potential allies and supporters and confirmed Lélia Gonzalez's view that certain forms of radical Black activism and theorizing were not able to understand other forms of Black resistance. As a national organization in the making, MNU attempted to cast a wide net in order to reach out and attract Black organizations that were not explicitly political, making a serious effort to create more space for culture as an aspect of its organizing platform. Additionally, MNU made a conscious effort to tone down its left-leaning rhetoric, and at its first Congress held in Rio de Janeiro in December of 1979, it changed the term from "struggle centers" to "action centers" in an effort to attract allies from poor backgrounds who perhaps feared associating with such radical-sounding units (Alberto 2011, 292).

The Movimento Negro Unificado in Salvador

MNU arrived in Salvador at a time of increasing Black consciousness and mobilization. With their founding in 1978, the bloco Ilê Aiyê was already four years old, and Olodum was founded a year later. As a newly emergent Black antiracist group MNU had to confront a series of deeply entrenched glaring social and political contradictions. Salvador in the late 1970s and early 1980s presented MNU with a ripe social scenario and an intriguing case study for Black social mobilization and grassroots action based on the following: first, the demographics of a Black majority population with a low economic standing that was completely excluded from economic and political power; second, the fact that along with the blocos there was a burgeoning Black consciousness movement and active neighborhood associations already fighting against the dictatorship in the early 1970s; third, the rise of a new class of Black candidates for political office (1980s and early 1990s); and fourth, the radical new forms of cultural politics being articulated by the blocos. These factors converged as MNU established itself in Salvador in the late 1970s and early 1980s.

In Salvador, the struggle against racial oppression historically had taken place mainly through organizations based on ethnic or cultural rather than explicitly racial identifications (Alberto 2011, 282). In the 1970s, slightly before the arrival of Ilê Aiyê, there were grassroots resistance organizations and neighborhood groups active across the city of Salvador. Given the prohibitions against open dissent, some of these groups worked as underground organizations with strong left-leaning tendencies, and some of their members would play an early and pivotal role in establishing the MNU chapter in Salvador. Groups like the secondary student movement CABRA (founded in 1974), the October 8 movement (founded in 1977), and the Joint Work of the Neighborhood (JWN) (founded in 1978) were active in Salvador's poorer communities before the arrival of MNU. These militant groups—erased from the so-cial movement history of Salvador—organized against the dictatorship in the early to mid-1970s. According to Valdíseo Fernandes, a long-time activist and ex–party militant of the Workers' Party (PT), these groups led the way and laid the foundations for MNU, predating Ilê Aiyê. Fernandes argues that these groups were also the precursors to the blocos and the modern Black consciousness movement in Salva-dor and MNU. Fernandes worked alongside Luiz Alberto, a founding member of MNU—who later became a federal deputy—as one of the key militants in JWN (Fernandes 2013).

Composed mainly of neighborhood groups with left-leaning mem-bers, they (the secondary student movement and October 8) empha-sized the high cost of living, lack of education, and poor health services in their communities. Their headquarters was located in the commu-nity of Alto de Peru, which later became the very first headquarters of MNU in Salvador. However, what Fernandes emphasizes about Salva-dor in the 1970s is that there were no explicitly organized Black politi-cal movements that directly articulated the issues of Black people at this time. It was groups like CABRA, the October 8 movement, and the Joint Work of the Neighborhood (JWN 1978) who, before MNU, first started to link poverty to racism and to larger structures of so-cial discrimination. These early groups mainly working on neighbor-hood issues were leftist in orientation and provided the foundations for groups like MNU and the blocos. These groups and their members would also later form the backbone of the Workers' Party in Salvador once it was established in the 1980s.

In July of 1978, Lélia González and Abdias do Nascimento visited Salvador to help recruit members, update supporters on plans, and assist in establishing a MNU chapter in Salvador. As respected activists and intellectuals they both had deep ties to Salvador's activist commu-nity based on their history as movement leaders. This visit led to one of the first MNU chapters being established in Salvador (Covin 2006, 74). Some of the founding or early members of the Salvador chapter include Luiz Alberto, Gilberto Leal, Ana Cristina, Wilson Santana, Raymondo Santos, and Jonathan Conceição. After the formation of

MNU, it was later decided that the Second National Assembly would be held in Salvador on November 4, 1979. It was at this assembly that the idea of a National Day of Black Consciousness was first discussed.

The cultural group Nego, mainly composed of Black activists, student groups, and musicians, served as the foundation for MNU activities and played a decisive role in the establishment of MNU in Salvador. Nego later transformed itself into the official MNU chapter. Nego as well as former members of the Secondary Student Movement CABRA, the October 8 movement, and the Joint Work of the Neighborhood morphed into the modern MNU. "Nego" later became the name of the official bulletin of MNU in Salvador, publishing essays and editorials on the Black problem in Brazil (Covin 2006, 101) and in May of 1987 *Nego* was adopted by MNU as its official newspaper. By the later 1980s and early 1990s the Salvador chapter had become one of MNU's leading sections as it furnished the core of the organization's national leadership and to some extent it set the national agenda (Covin 2006, 129). While exact numbers are difficult to gauge, it is estimated that during this period the MNU chapter in Salvador had roughly forty core activists with two hundred affiliated members. By the early 1980s, the Salvador chapter of MNU had moved from Alto de Peru and later relocated to Liberdade, where it remains today.

Gender, MNU, and Black Social Movements

The geometry of race and gender politics as points of intersection represented fault lines and on some level was deeply problematic in both the white-leaning feminist organizations and male-led Afro–social movements in Brazil in the 1970s and 1980s. The politics of race and gender proved difficult for many Black and women groups. Brazilian feminists did not prioritize race, largely for two reasons: First, the central debate in the 1970s and 1980s for Brazilian feminists was traditional Marxist orthodoxy of class analysis. In this framework, class dynamics were viewed as central whereas race was secondary. Second, like much traditional thinking during this time, the Brazilian feminist approach to racial discrimination stood in the deep shadows and was influenced by the ideas of racial democracy (Lovell 2000,

139). Afro-Brazilian women were caught in the crosscurrents of these prevailing hegemonies and therefore did not have the social space in traditional feminist structures to address racial inequality, nor did they have the space in the mainly male-led Afro–social movements to address gender. This conundrum led Afro-Brazilian women to develop social strategies and methodologies to deal with race and gender as intersectional and overlapping categories.

The calculus of race and gender dynamics as specific forms of social oppression arose as key social organizing ideas and gained traction in the early 1990s. Gender as a specific form of oppression and inequality became one of the defining issues that Black women's movement activists had to address. According to Lia Caldwell, while Black women historically composed a larger portion of the active membership of many Black organizations in major cities like São Paulo, Rio de Janeiro, and Salvador, Black men traditionally dominated the leadership of most organizations (Caldwell 2007, 155). Caldwell posits that sexism became a serious issue within the Black women's movement during the late 1970s and 1980s. A sense of displacement and alienation was felt by many Black women who were active in the 1980s. Many Black women were confined to the role of doing behind-the-scenes work and were limited in their access to leadership. Black women activists a faced a double-edged sword and dual fight in their larger struggle to deal with racialization and gender inequality. According to Caldwell, concerns about race were largely ignored by white Brazilian women's organizations and issues of gender were marginalized within the male-dominated Black movement (Caldwell 2007, 155). One woman activist expressed the following: "It is clear that the Black movement, like any other movement, is not immune to the effects of machismo and sexism" (Caldwell 2007).

In the late 1980s, Luiza Bairros, a well-known activist and respected leader of MNU from the Salvador chapter, commented on the huge difference between the discourses of the Black movement, which was based on the exaltation of Black women, and the sexist practices of Black men (Ribeiro 1995). The subordinate status of women in MNU, according to Bairros, stemmed from what Black male leaders saw as competition from women and the idea that male power and space should not be challenged (Ribeiro 1995). Caldwell posits that Black women's experiences and identities were profoundly shaped by racial and gender inequalities and therefore that as Black women they had a unique responsibility to respond to and frame issues based on the intersection of race and gender.

Black women, who found themselves increasingly marginalized in the women's and Black movements, responded by creating their own organizations and establishing special sections within existing organizations (Caldwell 2007, 155). Caldwell points out that while the Black movement was taking root in the 1980s, Black women, given the contradictions surrounding gender politics, were at the same time spearheading, founding, and organizing Black women's movements and organizations, a point not covered with much depth in much of the literature pertaining to Afro–social movements in Brazil. By calling attention to Black women and gender, Caldwell provides a finer lens with which to theorize and better understand the depth and breadth of Black social movements in Brazil. The struggle of Black women, as well as gender and race, is therefore central to theorizing and understanding the matrix of social oppression in Brazil.

Along these lines MNU spearheaded many important projects, one being in the area of race, gender, and education, with its Black Women's Front, which focused on grassroots education and human rights. Founding MNU member Ariana Cristina, a professor and actress from Salvador, played a pivotal role in establishing the Black Women's Front within MNU. Some of the women in Salvador argued that there was too much focus on political protest and demonstrations of solidarity to the detriment of the long-term transformational goals of education. The MNU women, therefore, created the Black Women's Front and organized adult education classes based on the pedagogy of Paulo Freire. The women of MNU recognized and addressed the multiple forms of oppression faced by Afro-Brazilian women and broadened the movement's agenda to include projects geared toward addressing gender inequality (Davis 1995, 260). While many issues remained the same—social discrimination, racism, lack of employment, and low salaries—the 1980s and 1990s brought a different focus. With the process of political liberalization and the new opening, issues of police brutality, lack of health care, violence against women, the rights of children, and the right of religious expression were addressed. In the 1990s, in one of its most ambitious projects, MNU tried to organize Black female domestic workers of Salvador; however, it was not a success.

MNU's Black Political Project

In the early 1990s MNU launched its Black Political Project, aimed at getting more Blacks elected to municipal office. Given the low number of Blacks in formal electoral politics there was a conscious effort and strategy to encourage Blacks to run for local and national office. MNU encouraged and endorsed Afro-Brazilians to run for political office through alliances with leftist parties by supporting candidates for municipal office in Salvador and Rio de Janeiro. Two of the key parties were the Democratic Labor Party (Partido Democrático Trabalhistas, or PDT) and the Workers' Party (PT). In 1992, MNU supported Luiz Alberto's candidacy for city council in Salvador, Jurema Batista for city council in Rio de Janeiro, and Benedita da Silva's historic candidacy for mayor of Rio de Janeiro (Covin 2006, 131). Da Silva was not elected mayor of Rio de Janeiro, but she made history as the first Black woman to run for the office. Da Silva had already served on Rio's city council from 1982 to 1987.

Jurema Batista was elected to Rio's city council and Alberto was unsuccessful in his run for city council; however, he would later be elected as federal deputy, where he currently serves. During this period, in the early 1990s, there was a rise of Black candidates seeking office in Salvador and across Brazil, and MNU played a key role in these processes. MNU's political campaigns and entrance into electoral politics, while significant, did not produce the mass base of support that its members had envisioned, as few candidates were elected. However, this campaign set the stage and provided a platform for future Black candidates seeking office on the local level in Salvador.

Suely Santos, a member of Salvador's MNU chapter since 1994, believes that the social base of Salvador's MNU militants was mainly left-leaning Workers' Party members and middle-class urban intellectuals. Philosophically they fused currents of Afrocentrism, Marxism, and Pan-Africanism into an eclectic frame of reference for analyzing the social situation of Blacks in Brazil (Santos 2013). For those who were both MNU and PT members there was an understanding that race analysis was central to understanding the status of Blacks in Brazil, a position not readily embraced by white members of the PT during this time. MNU members (like the Afro-Brazilian women in Black and feminist organizations) thus had two extremely difficult fights: first they had to "fight within the PT" to convince the rank-and-file members that the concept of racialization was an important organizing category; second they had to convince the Black masses that many of the problems in Salvador (and Brazil) were rooted in centuries of racialized discriminatory practices as well as develop a credible plan of action.

In Salvador, MNU was never a political party even though it did enter into politics and many of its members belonged to the Workers' Party; nor was it a mass organization of the working class, as most of its members came from the urban middle class. It was mainly organized as a diverse set of groups composed of many different organizations, and it has been described as a "unified Black movement," one in which many organizations were joined together and united explicitly around goals, objectives, and strategies to be defined in meetings, national assemblies, and congresses. Their purpose was to form a national movement to mobilize Afro-Brazilians to struggle for their collective well-being. MNU would be the first national Black organization to arise out of the Black consciousness movement. Their main accomplishments in Salvador were:

- to place the struggle for racial and gender equality (i.e., the fight against Black oppression and racial discrimination) on the social agenda and to make racism an important political issue for civil society and the state;
- to provide a methodology with which to frame Black social consciousness around social, political, and economic inequality;
- to fight within the Workers' Party to approach issues of race with a more critical lens and to promote Blacks within the party;

- to support Blacks for political office through its Black Political Project;
- to organize the Black Women's Front in some of Salvador's poorest communities;
- to first establish the ideas as well as organize and celebrate a national day for the Afro-leader Zumbi;
- to spearhead the campaign to teach African and Black history in public schools known as Law 10639, which would require public schools to teach African and Afro-Brazilian history;
- to publish the bulletin *Nego* and later a newspaper; and
- to frame some of the early debates around affirmative action.

By the late 1990s and early 2000s, at last, the Brazilian government finally had to admit that racism and racial discrimination were the social and political reality. Its seventh periodic report reads,

> For many decades, the myth of a nationality characterized by the harmonious and perfect fusion of three races, responsible for the construction of a "racial democracy" in the country, was propagated. Over a long period of time, the Brazilian State and society, acting on behalf of this myth, revealed themselves incapable of implementing effective mechanisms to incorporate Afro-descendants, indigenous individuals, and members of other discriminated groups into the larger society. The consequences of this process are reflected in this report and are evidence not only of the existence of racism in Brazil but of its cumulative effects in producing economic and social inequality. (United Nations Committee on the Elimination of Racial Discrimination 2003)

Such an admission in the context of Brazil is noteworthy, and MNU as well as many other Black groups were central to this hegemonic repositioning of racial discourse.

In fact, between the abolition of slavery in 1888, when the state claimed there was no racism, and 2003, when the government declared racism as social reality, were 113 long, grinding years. MNU and other Black groups therefore must be credited with putting an inordinate amount of pressure on the state to finally recognize processes of racialization and the historical impact of racialized social inequality as a legitimate and serious issue to be addressed. It was only through years of social action that MNU was able to "flip the script" and in doing so it made the "invisible" visible. Throughout Brazil's long racial history, the state had continuously denied racial discrimination or was guilty of, as one activist put it, "the deracialization of slavery and history." However, MNU made racialization visible within the social structure by providing a lens with which to analyze and better understand the mechanics of racial discrimination and the metrics of racism. It is against this backdrop that MNU's contribution to Black cultural politics should be seen.

MNU, while still active across the city, faces a deep crisis of identity, mission, and purpose. Unlike the early days, when there were very few groups focused on racial discrimination, over the two last decades the landscape has shifted and is now full of social organizations, NGOs, and religious groups doing similar work across Salvador and Brazil. MNU is still widely respected and is an important marker for some groups, but it is now one of many such groups operating in Salvador. It has not, however, entered into the lucrative networks or root tourism commodification like so many Black groups in Salvador: it has remained a small, independent grassroots organization committed to the recovery of Black identity and dignity in Salvador and across Brazil.

Affirmative Action and Education in Brazil

This chapter addresses the polemical debates surrounding the struggle for equality, civil rights, and specifically affirmative action laws in Brazil from the 1930s to the present. This historical time frame is important as it provides a perspective on how Afro–civil society groups have sought justice by arguing that the country's educational institutions were de facto racist and socially rigged against Black, indigenous, and poor Brazilians. Starting in the mid-1990s affirmative action in higher education gained traction and emerged as a key strategic issue for both Afro–civil society and the Brazilian government; by the early 2000s, a wide range of affirmative action policies had been adopted, and these developments were directly related to the decades of mobilization and arduous labor by Afro–civil society groups that had put unrelenting pressure on the Brazilian government.

Afro-groups and Black politicians had long called for measures to address the lack of Blacks in the Brazilian university system, the poor quality of public education, and the low position and status of Blacks in the labor market. These debates and discussions in the context of Afro–civil society social movements led to important policy changes resulting in the implementation of affirmative action programs across Brazil and therefore represented a radical paradigm shift in social and political relations (Martins, Medeiros, and Nascimento 2004). When former president Fernando Cardoso opened public discussions surrounding affirmative action in 1996, he opened a Pandora's box of gritty social questions leading to deep reflections and complex debates on the uneasy intersection of race, social justice, education, and citizenship with respect to the status of Blacks and indigenous Brazilians. There were of course no easy or simple solutions, as these issues were deeply intertwined in Brazil's history and social structures (Hernández 2013).

By doing so he challenged the geometry of social relations that put many Brazilians in an extremely difficult and uncomfortable social situation: the fact that until recently in Brazil, it was considered impolitic to openly discuss racial inequality—that is, racism and racial discrimination—even though they were hidden in plain sight. Brazilians for most part during the twentieth century chose to ignore or downplay questions of racialization, as such issues remained texturally submerged and therefore off the radar screen. And they were rarely, if ever, discussed in the national context, nor had core issues of structural racial discrimination and their social impact on and repercussions for Afro-Brazilians been directly addressed. As chapter 2 highlighted, in 1888 with the demise of slavery, Afro-Brazilians relocated from the plantation to the favelas (slums), and there was no federal assistance to aid ex-slaves, nor were there any special programs established to cushion the transition from slavery to freedom. However, the supreme and cruel irony was that in the aftermath of slavery, Brazil immediately declared itself free of racial discrimination: it was in fact an attempt to texturally submerge or deracialize a deeply racialized society and also to socially cleanse slavery from the institutional memory of Brazilian social relations.

With Cardoso's initiatives, along with the years of hard work and agitation by Afro–civil society groups, Brazilians from all strata of life now had to face a series of vexing and thorny questions that had been theretofore texturally submerged for decades if not centuries. These included the following: How had past and current forms of racial discrimination structured the life chances and opportunities of Afro-Brazilians? What role does racial inequality play in determining who goes to the university, where one lives, and what position one occupies in the political economy? More important, by opening the discussion,

Cardoso more or less admitted that Blacks had been the historical victims of deeply embedded forms of structural racialized social discrimination. This admission, while perhaps not noteworthy from a North American racial perspective, represented a radical paradigm shift in Brazilian social relations; theretofore Brazilian society had vigorously defended itself as a unique "racial paradise" bereft of racial discrimination. The winds of social change were now sweeping across the nation, and many complex questions regarding the place, status, and rights of Afro-Brazilians had to be squarely addressed.

Overview of Affirmative Action in Brazil

By the middle of the 1990s and the start of the 2000s there were social movements, forces, and events rapidly unfolding that reaffirmed, however unevenly, Afro–civil society's and Black movements' demands for affirmative action. Some of these forces include—but are not limited to—the following: the early initiative of Fernando Henrique Cardoso regarding affirmative action (Telles 2004, 204); the adoption of affirmative action by the Federal University of Rio de Janeiro in 2000 and 2001 (Lima 2012); the election of Ignacio Lula da Silva in 2002; the decision by Lula in 2003 to appoint Joaquim Barbosa (de Brito 2013), that is, the first Black to serve on the Supremo Tribunal Federal (Brazilian Supreme Court), who served as the chief justice from 2012 to 2014; and the enactment of a federal scholarship program in 2005 aimed at poor, Black, and indigenous students, the University for All Program (Pro-Uni) (Lima 2012). Finally, on the international level the World Conference against Racism held in Durban, South Africa, in 2001 represented another defining event that reverberated positively and provided a turbo boost to the proponents of affirmative action (dos Santos 2010). Collectively these actions were watershed moments, as they ushered in a new social landscape and radically new ways of thinking about racial discrimination because they were designed to strengthen and advance affirmative action initiatives in education. These events set in motion a new set of social relations.

The year 2012 also represented a decisive new stage that cemented the struggle for affirmative action in Brazil: first there were two groundbreaking constitutional rulings by the Brazilian Supreme Court (Lima 2012; Hernández 2013), and second, a comprehensive law known as the Law of Social Quotas was signed and enacted by President Rousseff (Romero 2012). In April of 2012, the Brazilian Supreme Court in a historic case ruled 10–0 in favor of affirmative action regarding admission policies at the University of Brasília and the University of Rio do Sol. The court ruled that affirmative action is a constitutionally valid social policy (Hernández 2013). And in May of 2012, the Brazilian Supreme Court, in another very important legal case, ruled in favor and confirmed the constitutionality of Pro-Uni (Lima 2012). In these two groundbreaking legal rulings the Brazilian Supreme Court affirmed the constitutional priority of reducing social inequalities and the use of affirmative action as an important tool of social integration (Hernández 2013, 157). Afro–civil society groups and other advocates believe that these are some of the most important Supreme Court decisions to address affirmative action and racial inequality in Brazil.

Along with these two important legal victories, in August of 2012, President Dilma Rousseff signed the Law of Social Quotas, which requires all federal universities to reserve at least 50 percent of their seats for Black and indigenous students. The first phase of the law went into effect in October of 2012, requiring federal universities to first reserve at least 12.5 percent of seats each for both public high school graduates and Black, brown, and indigenous students. By 2016, public universities will be required to increase the percentage to 50 percent (Romero 2012). According to the sixth article of the law, the Ministry of Education and the Secretariat for Policies to Promote Racial Equality are the key institutions in charge of monitoring and assessing the program as well as implementing it; it (the Secretariat for Policies to Promote Racial Equality) is also required to consult with the National Foundation for the Indigenous (FUNAI). The two Supreme Court decisions and the new Law of Social Quotas have inevitably led to discussions about the relevancy and significance of affirmative action, racial quotas, and racial discrimination, resulting in hot debates across the country. The Law of Social Quotas takes the previous affirmative action policies to another level. The minister in charge of Brazil's Secretariat for Policies to Promote Racial Equality, Mrs. Luiza Bairros, in an interview with the *New York Times*, said that officials expect the number of Black and indigenous students admitted to the federal universities to climb to 56,000 from 8,700 in the coming years (Romero 2012). According to Tanya Hernández, a legal scholar who has studied comparative anti-discrimination laws aimed at Afro-Latin populations in the Americas, given their scope and depth, Brazil's affirmative action laws—and by extension the Law of Social Quotas—are possibly the most comprehensive affirmative action laws in the Americas—including the United States (Hernández 2013, 151).

These historical events have long social trajectories and have marinated in Brazilian social relations throughout the twentieth century. However, with the end of authoritarian rule toward the last half of the twentieth century and the reemergence of Afro–civil society in the 1970s and 1980s, the idea of racial democracy as a hegemonic project was challenged and effectively deconstructed. This chapter addresses the following questions: What is the proper historical context for understanding debates about affirmative action in Brazil? What role did Afro–civil society play in placing affirmative action squarely on the table and how did they reposition key debates on racial justice? And what are some of the key debates and discussions regarding the relative merits of affirmative action? Since affirmative action was one of the principal demands of Afro–civil society groups, the new law and recent Supreme Court decisions, at least on the surface, appear to be significant victories. However, there are many currents within these debates that need to be teased out.

This chapter aims to frame affirmative action debates and does not attempt to evaluate these new affirmative action programs, university admission policies, student test scores, the implementation protocols of universities, or the success rate of the first wave of affirmative action applications. While these are of course important questions, they will be dealt with in future research as more data becomes available. This chapter aims to shed light and position the reader's understanding of some of the more burning questions by, first, exploring many of the ideas and debates central to understanding the role of Afro–civil society in changing the calculus of social relations on questions of racial equality and by, second, providing a context with which to see the social evolution of affirmative action in modern Brazil. It will untangle and situate these debates within the broader racial discourses (historical and contemporary) and the struggle for social justice in Brazil and Salvador. With this aim the reader will be able to arrive at his or her own conclusions regarding the role of affirmative action in Brazil and larger strategic questions regarding remedies aimed at addressing racial inequality.

The Historical Trajectory of Early Civil Rights and Affirmative Action, 1930s to the Present

The idea of affirmative action and other special measures designed to counter injustices against the Afro-Brazilian masses has its roots in Afro–civil society and Black social movements starting in the 1930s and 1940s. During this time a number of important Afro–civil society and political organizations emerged not only to counter and challenge racial inequality but also to articulate a more positive meaning of Blackness. While affirmative action was not always explicitly included in their demands in the 1930s and 1940s, it was the overall struggle against racial discrimination and oppression by Afro-Brazilians that defined their more explicit human rights agenda. However, access to fair and just education was always one of the core organizing principles for Black groups in the 1930s and 1940s, including two early groups, the Frente Negra Brasileira (FNB / Black Brazilian Front) and Teatro Experimenta do Negro (TEN / Black Experimental Theater), whose origins date back to that time. These two pioneering civil society groups organized around issues of civil rights, education, Black identity, Black aesthetics, and Black art.

Brazil's first race-specific political activist organization was the Centro Civic Palmares, founded in 1926 in São Paulo. Its main aim was to mobilize the Black community around human and civil rights, and in 1931 its former members went on to create the FNB (Nascimento 2007, 122). The FNB, building on the work of the Centro Civic Palmares, was founded in September of 1931 for the purpose of unifying the network of Black liberation organizations that already existed in several regions of the country. The FNB is believed to be one of the first

Afro-Brazilian groups to fight for civil rights during this period. It was the largest and most active organization at the time with an estimated membership of seventy thousand, and as part of a mass-based protest movement it fought against racial discrimination and the exclusion of Blacks from trade unions and the industrial economy (Rodrigues da Silva 2012, 188). It was located in several important cities across Brazil—including Salvador—and one of its key organizing principles was to protest the targeted exclusion of Blacks from employment and the education system as well as the segregation policies of movie theaters, barber shops, hotels, restaurants, and other public places that refused service to Blacks. It also operated its own school, as one of its key goals was educating Blacks (Nascimento 2007, 128). The FNB had a school for children in its headquarters with teachers appointed by the government, and it offered literacy courses and adult education classes.

The FNB used the term "negro" (Black) after 1931—unheard of and unprecedented for this time—and it used the term aggressively. Its journal, *Voz da Raça* (the voice of the race), founded in 1933, challenged the basic tenets of racial democracy with phrases like "color prejudice, in Brazil, is something only we Blacks can feel" (Butler 2000, 57). *Voz da Raça* was also used as an organizing tool by the FNB to communicate with its membership base and make calls to action. As an integrationist organization its main aim was to build and strengthen ties and influence the political process. According to the FNB, civil rights meant equal treatment under the law and the right to work free of discrimination (Davis 2000, 255). It registered as a political party in 1936, making it one of the only Black political parties in Brazil during this time. It maintained its headquarters in São Paulo but had an important presence in Salvador and Minas Gerais as well as in other states. Kim Butler labels FNB's approach "alternative integration" since their aim was to include Blacks as part of society by using alternative approaches (Butler 2000, 217). The FNB openly attacked color prejudice using marches and demonstrations, cultivated and encouraged race pride among Blacks, fought against apathy and indifference within the Black community, and sought to teach or reeducate whites about the Black contribution to Brazilian identity (Davis 2007, 184). During its six years of existence from 1931 to 1937, it was able to mobilize thousands in parades, street demonstrations, public conferences, and seminars, all of which focused on racial discrimination against Blacks.

FNB organizers were early pioneers in the area of civil rights and Black social mobilization. They demanded social equality for Afro-Brazilians and were instrumental in getting an antiracism clause incorporated into the 1934 constitution. However, in 1937 the FNB was outlawed along with other groups under Gertulio Vargas's Estado Novo (New State), which banned all political organizations. The ban on the FNB and its demise was a major blow to Afro-Brazilians, as it was one of few political outlets available during this time, and some activists from the period believe that Afro-Brazilians actually lost ground (Hanchard 1994, 105). However, FNB's labor paved the way for the inevitable struggle around Black rights and early antidiscrimination legislation. It was the most significant articulation of Black demands and social consciousness during this time.

With the demise of the FNB toward the end of the 1930s, other groups emerged to fill the vacuum. One was the Teatro Experimenta do Negro. Founded in 1944 and first organized by Abdias do Nascimento, TEN sought to combat racism in general and the exclusion of Blacks in theater in particular. It was mainly organized as a Black arts theatrical company but evolved to do more cultural and political work after its founding (Martins, Medeiros, and Nascimento 2004, 791). Equally important is that in the 1940s and 1950s it began to develop and express early ideas regarding affirmative action for Blacks. For example, it called for free schooling for all Brazilian children as well as subsidized admission of Black students to secondary schools and universities while waging a relentless fight against racism through cultural and educational programs (Martins, Medeiros, and Nascimento 2004, 791). Much of TEN's work concentrated on the arts; however, it placed a high premium on cultivating an intellectual Black elite, or talented tenth, by promoting education for Blacks, thus its early emphasis on affirmative action. According to TEN, it was only through education that Blacks would be able to break down the thick invisible walls of social discrimination and challenge the reproduction of social inequality in education, the arts, the political system, and the labor market.

In 1951, the Brazilian legislature passed the first antidiscrimination measure, known as the Afonso Arinos law (Lei Numero 1.390, June 1951). Despite the low social status of Afro-Brazilians and their day-to-day oppression, and despite the work of groups like FNB and TEN, the Afonso Arinos law was enacted only after two African American women visiting Brazil were barred from entering hotels in Rio de Janeiro and São Paulo: in 1947, Irene Diggs was refused entrance into the Hotel Serrador in Rio de Janeiro, and in 1950, Katherine Dunham was barred from entering Hotel Espland; both were denied entry because of their skin color (Alberto 2011, 175). These events, widely covered by the press, caused serious embarrassment to Brazil's ruling elite, and in the minds of Black activists they only reinforced the idea that racism was pervasive across Brazil.

The mistreatment of Diggs and Dunham due to skin color ignited a hot national and international debate, leading the Brazilian congress to enact the antidiscrimination Afonso Arinos law of 1951. The law, while weak and rarely enforced, provided for a series of punishments for public and private establishments that refused service to people of color, including a fine and up to a year in prison. Repeat offenders could lose their positions and their establishments could be shut down (Alberto 2011, 177). However, the law, despite its origins, did not openly acknowledge Brazil's racism, nor did it seek to address it even though it was Afro–civil society justice groups that organized around the Katherine Dunham incident by publicizing it to both the media and the public. In the forty-six-year period following its enactment, only nine people were convicted of racial discrimination (Cesar 2003, 212–13).

According to historian Paulina Alberto, what has gone relatively unnoticed about the law's bizarre history and enactment is the extent to which it was the result of the efforts by Afro-Brazilian activists to make political democracy a vehicle for racial equality during this period (Alberto 2011, 178). Equally important is that there were savvy Afro–civil society groups that were instrumental in keeping pressure on the government to address racial discrimination in public accommodations. However, what is quite disturbing regarding the logic of the Arinos law is that it clearly privileged racial discrimination against two foreigners over that against its own citizens: the Brazilian government, always image-conscious, was motivated into action only when two African-descended women from the United States were the recipients of racial discrimination and humiliation. The objective fact that many Afro-Brazilians faced day-to-day racial discrimination, social exclusion, and denial of basic service in many public accommodations was not important and only secondary to the law's main aim. Many Afro-groups in Brazil had long urged the government to do more to address racial mistreatment in public accommodations to no avail.

As early as 1946, Black activists as well as Gilberto Freyre (a congressman at the time) called for an antidiscrimination clause in the 1946 constitution. In fact the Arinos law was a diluted version of a 1946 antidiscrimination bill that Afro-Brazilian activists had tried to introduce (Nascimento 2007, 61). Examining the larger strategic context of Black social activism in the late 1940s and early 1950s spotlights the way these groups attempted to harness racial democracy as core components of democracy and citizenship in Brazil (Romo 2010, 178). At this time the demand for affirmative action programs did not gain traction, but it would resurface by the late twentieth century as part of a powerful argument used by a broad array of Afro–civil society groups across Brazil. With the emergence of the military dictatorship, or the silent revolution of 1964, all alternative political groups were outlawed and repressed (much like during the Vargas regime of the 1930s). Starting in 1964 with the rise of the dictatorship scores of activists were jailed as the regime tightened its reign, and thousands were tortured and disappeared. During the period of the dictatorship (1964 to 1985) antidiscrimination laws were largely unenforced and were not taken very seriously. Black movement groups and many of their demands for racial justice and affirmative action were structurally silenced, and such demands would not resurface until the middle of the 1970s. However, by the 1970s, when Afro–civil society groups resurfaced, they assumed a more robust, vibrant, and militant posture.

Against this backdrop, for decades Afro–civil society groups have had a number of tasks before them: first, to challenge and discredit the tenets of racial democracy as a hegemonic project; second, to understand the various platforms of social oppression and discrimination;

third, to create new ways of conceptualizing the multiple forms of Blackness; fourth, to develop concrete programs of political action and grassroots mobilization; and fifth, to clearly articulate all of the above and deal with racial discrimination and its legacy as well as translate them into concrete political projects. Affirmative action is one of the concrete gains of Afro–civil society, and notwithstanding some of the problems associated with race-based solutions, it does represent a step forward in addressing racial discrimination and its horrid legacy.

The 1980s: The Return to Democracy and Early Affirmative Action

As discussed in the introduction and chapters 3 and 4, the middle of the 1970s and the start of the 1980s witnessed the flourishing of democracy and civil society in Brazil after two decades of brutal dictatorial rule. Starting in 1982 there were competitive multiparty elections, and in 1985 José Sarney became the first civilian president in twenty years. The year 1988 marked a new beginning, and after extensive consultations, a new federal constitution was written. The return to democracy in 1985, the enactment of the new federal constitution in 1988, and the continued rise of Afro–civil groups created new political spaces in which to frame and articulate Black rights, focusing on education, jobs, and land rights. In the brief period between 1982 and 1988, Brazil defined racism as a crime, reaffirmed itself as a multicultural state, committed itself to protecting Afro-Brazilian cultural practices, and created mechanisms through which titles could be granted to quilombo communities (United Nations Committee on the Elimination of Racial Discrimination 2003).

Abdias do Nascimento, an activist from the 1940s and the founder of TEN, successfully ran and won a seat in the first post-dictatorship congressional elections of 1982 and took office in 1983 as one of the first Afro-Brazilians to defend his community in the national legislature. Wasting no time, he immediately introduced comprehensive antidiscrimination legislation and one of the first bills proposing affirmative action. Unimaginable at the time and as countercurrent to the prevailing hegemonies, Law Number (Bill) 1.332/83 called for "compensatory action to implement the rights of equal opportunity and equal protection . . . secured by article 153, section 1 of the Constitution." The bill proposed a set of compensatory measures in education, government, employment, and civil service, including incentives for diversity programs in the private sector. It set goals of 20 percent Black women and 20 percent Black men (40 percent total) in all agencies of public administration and at all levels of government (Martins, Medeiros, and Nascimento 2007, 793). Congressman Nascimento also introduced Bill PL 3.196/84 mandating that 40 percent of seats be reserved for Blacks in the prestigious Rio Branco Institute, Brazil's Ministry of Foreign Relation's diplomatic school (Martins, Medeiros, and Nascimento 2004, 794).

These measures were of course never passed, as the idea of affirmative action was not taken seriously and had not yet matured into a credible idea for mainstream politicians and civil society institutions in Brazil. However, the tide was turning and the currents of change were on the horizon, as the Brazilian congress did approve several measures proposed by Afro–civil society, which were included in the new constitution of 1988 (specifically, racism was defined as a crime, and Brazil reaffirmed itself as a multicultural state, committed itself to protecting Afro-Brazilian cultural practices, and created mechanisms to grant titles to quilombo communities) as mentioned previously. Thus with the return of democracy the current federal constitution was adopted in 1988, and Afro–civil society groups were instrumental in getting some important measures included related to racial discrimination as part of the new steps toward democratization. These measures, however slow and gradual, were symbolic but were precursors of the shifting landscape and the unfolding social changes to come.

By the middle of the 1990s, Afro–civil society groups continued to flourish, and a new affirmative action regime came to power that was favorably inclined to Black social movement civil rights demands. In 1995 Fernando Henrique Cardoso took power, and his presidency marked another crucial turning point in Brazil's race relations and approach to Black rights. Important shifts occurred during Cardoso's tenure; he was perhaps the first Brazilian president to critically understand race, racial discrimination, and race-based social inequality.

His doctoral dissertation examined race relations, and he coauthored an important book and several articles on racial discrimination earlier in his career. As a sociologist, Cardoso along with Octavio Ianni published *Côr e mobilidade social em Florianópolis: Aspectos das relaçoes negros e brancos numa communidade do Brasil meridional* (Color and social mobility in Florianopolis: Aspects of relations between Blacks and whites in a southern Brazilian community). He therefore assumed the presidency schooled in the history of race in Brazil and was, as a result, critical at best and skeptical at worst of Brazil's past hypocrisy in denying racial discrimination.

Some important measures during his tenure were, first, that he created an Inter-ministerial Working Group to Valorize the Black Population; second, that the government submitted a human rights report to the United Nations Human Rights Committee that proclaimed affirmative action was compatible with Brazilian legislation and committed the state "to take positive measures to promote equality"; third, that a 1996 National Human Rights Program proposed specific policies aimed at providing support for Black-owned businesses with affirmative action programs and measures to increase access to universities; and, finally, that in 1996 the government organized an international seminar on affirmative action in Brazil (Htun 2004, 67). This new political space opened unique opportunities for greater civic engagement and empowered civil society actors to push for greater changes during his presidency (Htun 2004, 70). With these measures—to name only a few—it is argued that the affirmative action regime was now firmly in place.

The transition in the twentieth century of Brazilian state policy on race, according to Mala Htun, is best described as a transition from antidiscrimination in the 1930s and 1940s to affirmative action toward the end of the twentieth century and the start of the twenty-first century. She points out that these changes did not result from perceived electoral advantages on the part of politicians nor from material rewards for politicians but instead came about due to the role of Afro–civil society organizations and researchers who had argued for years that racism in Brazil was a structural social reality and racial inequality had to be directly addressed (Htun 2004, 75). In the modern period (after 1982) it was the role of Afro–civil society groups, the transition to democracy and the new constitution, the presidencies of Cardoso and Lula da Silva, and the World Conference against Racism that ushered in modern-day affirmative action.

The World Conference against Racism held in Durban, South Africa, in 2001 served to positively reinforce the ideas and demands of Afro–civil groups for racial justice. The Brazilian government worked together with civil society groups composed of grassroots activists and labor and religious leaders, as well as with other groups, in order to prepare for the conference and participate in a series of preparatory sessions regionally and nationally. For instance, the regional prep session was held in Chile in 2000 (Telles 2004, 68). The national prep session, one of Brazil's first national modern conferences against racism and intolerance, was held in Rio de Janeiro and segued into the international conference to be held later, in Durban, in 2001. Chaired by Benedita da Silva, it brought together more than 1,700 participants from around Brazil. The conference produced a report written by the preparatory committee and it endorsed quotas, antidiscrimination measures, and affirmative action (Telles 2004, 70).

What are important to note are the mutually reinforcing roles played by transnational advocacy networks, on one hand, and Afro–civil society in Brazil, on the other, as both placed an inordinate amount of pressure on the Brazilian government to take fairly advanced positions, such as making explicit commitments to the principle of compensatory policies for the Black populations. Transnational advocacy networks like the Latin American Caribbean Alliance brought together several hundred activists to the regional prep conference in Chile. And groups like Mundo Afro, the International Human Rights Law Groups, and the Ford Foundation were crucial in terms of building support for the Durban conference as they provided coordination, funding, training, and expertise in the area of international human rights (Telles 2004, 69–70).

The final document produced in Durban recommended affirmative action and other policies aimed at historically marginal groups and called for adequate representation in policies while underscoring the need for special measures for Afro-Brazilians and indigenous rights.

According to Htun, preparations for Durban stimulated civil mobilization, media interest, and most importantly public dialogue. Durban added a layer of legitimacy to Black demands and strengthened the moral position of affirmative action advocates (Htun 2004, 83). Moreover, transnational ideas articulated via networks of global civil society linked race to democracy, citizenship, and human rights. The Durban conference, by highlighting racial discrimination as a matter of human rights, served to place racial discrimination within a transnational frame based on the perspective of transnational civil society.

Affirmative Action Gains Traction: 2000 and Beyond

In 2000 the Ministry of Education issued a dismal report indicating that roughly 2 percent of all university students were Black (Carvalho 2001, 17), and more disturbing was that in elite and prestigious programs like medicine, law, and engineering, the proportion of Afro-Brazilians was much lower. The 2000s represented another decisive moment and turning point in higher education as more and more universities began to implement affirmative action programs in order to address the glaring disparities in Brazil's largely white educational utopia. In December 2000, Anthony Garotinho, governor of Rio de Janeiro, approved a local law reserving half of the available slots in undergraduate courses of public universities in Rio for students who had attended public schools (Lima 2012, 1). The next year in a follow-through to this law, on October 9, 2001, the Rio de Janeiro state legislature approved a bill establishing a quota of 40 percent for Blacks in the two state universities. In July 2002, the Federal University of Bahia in Salvador announced that 40 percent of spots in undergraduate and graduate programs would be reserved for Afro-Brazilians; and in November of 2002, the state legislature in Minas Gerais approved a 20 percent quota followed by the University of Brasília in 2003 (Htun 2004, 72).

At the same time there were other important social forces emerging during this period. The 2002 election saw the rise of Luiz Inácio da Silva, a charismatic trade unionist with humble origins from the Northeast of Brazil, a forward-thinking progressive who hailed from and identified with the poor and marginalized masses (Bourne 2008). The Northeast region, the poorest area of Brazil, known for its deep, grinding poverty and deep pockets of social inequality, is home to one of Brazil's highest concentrations of African-descended people—many of whom have had to migrate to the larger cities like Rio and São Paulo in search of better opportunities. Lula, possibly one of the most popular presidents in the modern history of the Americas, appointed Blacks to head key ministries and created the Secretariat for Policies Promoting Racial Inclusion (SEPPIR). SEPPIR, as an intergovernmental agency, is structured and organized to promote policy measures by means of task forces, the most important being the Racial Equality Institute, created in September of 2003; its policies are synchronized with those of the Ministry of Education. SEPPIR and the ministry jointly produced a report on national policy for the promotion of racial equality, which placed emphasis on affirmative action and quilombo community entitlements as well as a monitoring system allowing for the implementation of policies combating racial discrimination (Rodrigues da Silva 2012).

After Lula's election, he appointed three Afro-Brazilians to head key ministries, an act unprecedented in Brazilian politics. These included musician and megastar Gilberto Gil to head the Ministry of Culture; Benedita da Silva, a former senator and ex-governor from the state of Rio, to be minister for Social Assistance and Promotion; and Marina Silva, an environmentalist and former senator, to serve as minister of environment. Equally important, in 2003 Lula appointed an Afro-Brazilian, Joaquim Barbosa Gomes, to the Supremo Tribunal Federal (Brazilian Supreme Court), making him the first Black to serve on Brazil's top court in its 184 (plus)–year history. In October 2012, Barbosa was elected as the president of the court for a two-year term (de Brito 2013). Barbosa hails from humble origins and comes from the small town of Paracatu, located in the state of Minas Gerais, where his father worked as a bricklayer.

As a teenager, Barbosa moved to Brasília, finding work first as a janitor in a courtroom. The supreme irony flows as follows: Against all odds he was later admitted to the University of Brasília law program, one of the most prestigious schools in the country, and he was of course one of the only Black students in the program at the time. He later won admission to the distinguished Rio Branco institute, which trains diplomats, an institution he refers to "as one of the most discriminatory in Brazil." Trained in comparative law and fascinated by legal systems, he authored a book on affirmative action in the United States and is a strong admirer of Thurgood Marshall, the first African American appointed to the U.S. Supreme Court (Romero 2013). As a former prosecutor and diplomat, Barbosa is regarded as a progressive legal scholar with a brilliant mind who is an advocate of affirmative action and other mechanisms that address racial and social inequality. His appointment in 2003 as the first Black Supreme Court justice was historic and signaled a continued shift in the already changing social landscape. Moreover, the position of Supreme Court jurist in Brazil is extremely important because of its power and influence and because the term of office is guaranteed until the age of seventy.

Lula's forward-looking social policies and key ministerial and judicial appointments as well as the affirmative action programs established previously by the states of Rio de Janeiro, Bahia, Brasília, and Minas Gerais served to further strengthen the affirmative action regime and consolidate its institutional base. Moreover, throughout the 2000s affirmative action policies gained steam in policy circles and were incorporated by local governments and universities including the University of Brasília. However, there were legal issues brewing as these changes both radical and historic unsettled many across Brazil. Race and racial inequality took center stage, and after centuries of being texturally submerged, for better or worse, they were now in the social spotlight. There were of course tense debates on the merits of affirmative action and the role of the state in refereeing social justice. A glimpse into Brazil's educational system offers some clues into how educational and social opportunities are structured.

The Logic of Affirmative Action in Brazil

In order to best frame discussions around education and affirmative action in Brazil it is crucial to understand the following: the Brazilian public (primary and secondary) educational system is universally regarded as inferior and poorly funded. Those families who can afford it place their children in private primary and secondary schools, where they receive a far superior education. In stark contrast, Brazil's publicly funded federal university system is universally regarded as very prestigious and is held in high esteem, and for those who are admitted it cost very little to attend. However, in order to gain acceptance to a federal university (or any university) students are required to take the vestibular (college entrance exam) regardless of where they went to school, public or private. Moreover, students are strongly encouraged to take—before the actual vestibular exam—a prep course that prepares them for the main exam; however, prep courses are very expensive, and many Black and poor students simply cannot afford the high cost and usually do not take them and thus are put at a disadvantage with respect to students who can afford such costs. And the vestibular is known to be notoriously difficult to pass, and it is common for students to have to take it several times before finally passing (or receiving an acceptable score).

The logic of class relations and patterns of social inequality suggest the following: most upper-class students—almost always whites—attend private primary and secondary schools, where they receive superior preparation; meanwhile, most poor students—almost always Black, brown, and indigenous—attend public primary and secondary schools and receive a substandard, second-class education in schools that are underfunded and overcrowded with poorly trained teachers. However, as students prepare to enter the university—rich and poor, as well as white, Black, and brown—all are required to take the vestibular administered by the university they plan to attend. A student's score on the vestibular, and not their grade point average as in the United States, determines whether they are admitted. Evidence strongly indicates that students from private primary and secondary schools are better prepared academically to take the vestibular entrance exam— and score higher—whereas students from public primary and secondary schools are less prepared and have a greater difficulty passing it and so have more problems getting into the prestigious federal universities.

Affirmative action programs in education therefore specifically target and place emphasis on students who attend public primary and secondary schools—the vast majority of whom are Black, brown, and poor. The logic of class relations in the education system severely punishes Black and poor students, who attend poorly funded public schools while the well-financed, tuition-free federal university system rewards the predominantly white upper and upper-middle classes. The educational system thus becomes a primary site of class struggle as it serves to reproduce educational inequality simultaneously along the axes of race and class; it is against this backdrop that the current debates on affirmative action in Brazil have unfolded.

Legal and Constitutional Issues

In 2003 there was a legal challenge—and more were on the way—to race-based affirmative action programs. The State University of Rio de Janeiro (Universidade Estadual do Rio de Janeiro—UERJ) had its affirmative action policy challenged before the Federal Supreme Court and by several people and institutions: first a state legislator, second a group of disgruntled white students, and third a consortium of private schools. Roughly three hundred white students who were denied admission to UERJ went to the courts, and an injunction was imposed. The legal challenge, however, was later ruled moot when the state legislature was pressured to revise the policy (Hernández 2013). However, there were more challenges to come.

In 2009, in one of the most significant challenges to come before the Federal Supreme Court, a motion was filed by the Democrats (DEM), a center-right political party. The Democrats questioned the administrative acts of the Council of Teaching, Research, and Extension of the University of Brasília, which determined the number of reserved slots offered by the university. The party claimed that the quota policy adopted by the University of Brasília would undermine various fundamental precepts of Brazil's Federal Constitution. The University of Rio do Sol's affirmative action policies were also challenged in this case. These cases set the stage for the Brazilian Supreme Court to address the complex legal issues regarding the validity of affirmative action programs. While the winds of social change had swept across Brazil, it would be left up to the Supreme Court to clarify and codify important legal principles theretofore never addressed.

The main legal issue before the Federal Supreme Court was the contention that the affirmative action quota system violated a central constitutional principle of equality before the law, pursuant to Article 5 of the Brazilian constitution. Article 5 states, "All are equal before the law, without distinction of any nature, guaranteeing Brazilians and foreign residents in Brazil the inviolability of the right to life, liberty, equality, and property." Using Article 5 as the premise, white students who had been denied admission who had higher scores on the vestibular than other candidates who were accepted asserted that they were treated unfairly under such affirmative action policies. Their argument was that to treat one class of persons more favorably "based on race" was a direct violation of Article 5, which states all are "equal before the law" (González 2010, 127). Moreover, the legal briefs of the plaintiffs also argued that in Brazil there was no institutional racism and therefore that the imposition of affirmative action (on behalf of one group) is another form of racism. This argument follows along the trajectory of racial democracy—that is, it is claimed that because there is no (or never was any) discrimination against Black and brown populations, affirmative action programs for one group by definition disadvantage another group, specifically whites.

According to this line of thinking, "equality" is functionally equivalent to equal treatment, thus ignoring and negating historically inscribed forms of past social discrimination (González 2010, 128). In other words, if, as the plaintiffs suggest, there has been no past racial discrimination, then such factors as race should not be relevant to who gets into the university. Central to this line of reasoning is the meaning of justice and the role of the state in arbitrating structurally based class, racial, and gender inequalities. In the Brazilian legal context the argument is that constitutional guarantees of social equality of the individual—that is, Article 5—ought to be interpreted to mean that any differential treatment to favor one group is unconstitutional and not permitted. Therefore, setting aside seats for specific groups based on race violates this core principle. In other words, the plaintiffs viewed affirmative action as a violation of the principle of equality, whereas its advocates—in sharp contrast—viewed it as a remedy to address past racial discrimination and thus a way to achieve social equilibrium, fairness, and, most important, racial justice. These are the issues the Supreme Court had to address.

On April 26, 2012, in one of the most closely watched cases in recent history, the Federal Supreme Court issued a stunning ruling that sent shock waves across Brazil: it found the Federal University of Brasìlia's affirmative action policy constitutionally valid and therefore legal. In a unanimous ruling (10–0) the Federal Supreme Court of Brazil stated that in the mandate for the state to effectuate the principle of equality, affirmative action policies are an important duty and social responsibility because the constitution requires reparations for the past losses imposed on Afro-Brazilians (Hernández 2013, 156). A week later, in another precedent-shattering ruling, it reaffirmed and upheld the constitutionality of Pro-Uni, a national scholarship program for Black and indigenous students.

The court considered in the first case the *ação de descumprimento de preceito fundamental* (ADPF 186), or denunciation of the fundamental precept of noncompliance, which was then challenged by the right-of-center party, the Democrats. In addition to this denunciation, there was a *recurso extraordinário* (RE 597285), or extraordinary appeal, which was brought by a student from the Federal University of Rio Grande do Sul (UFRGS) who was eliminated from competition for one slot at the Federal University of Rio Grande do Sul despite having had higher scores on the vestibular than other candidates did. His elimination occurred due to the fact the University do Grande reserves 30 percent of its slots for candidates who attended public school and half of that quota for candidates who declare themselves "negros," or Afro-descendants, in their submissions.

The ruling of April 26 repudiated and rejected the claim of a student who said he was discriminated against when the Federal University of Rio do Sol rejected him in favor of Black students with lower entrance exam scores. The ruling also rejects the claim made by a Brazilian senator that racial quotas at the University of Brasília violate the principle of equality. In theory, the court's ruling, at least for now, will allow Brazilian universities to continue their efforts to mitigate the long history of social discrimination against Brazil's racially oppressed groups.

The justices on the court offered a number of important and insightful comments. According to Justice Ricardo Lewandowski, "it is not enough not to discriminate; it is necessary to facilitate. The stance should be, above all, affirmative action. It is necessary that this is the position taken by legislators. Neutrality has shown itself in these years to be a great failure." Along similar lines of argumentation, Justice Luis Fux said that race can and should be a political criterion of analysis for entry into a university as in many democratic countries. The construction of a fair and sympathetic society requires the whole community to repair past damages of our ancestors, according to Fux (de Jesus 2013).

Justice Rosa Weber, weighing in on how education structures opportunities in higher education and specifically speaking about the quota system, said, "If Blacks don't make it to the university, they do not share equal footing with whites, and . . . once Blacks reach a more equitable level then no such measures are needed" (de Jesus 2013). Justice Joaquim Barbosa, the only Black person on the court and an expert on affirmative action, argued eloquently that affirmative action policies aim to neutralize the pernicious effects of the brutal history of racial discrimination. He also added that he knows that those who have benefited from historical discrimination aimed at minorities tend to dislike affirmative action (de Jesus 2013).

What stands out in these opinions by the justices is their bold, daring, and straightforward thinking on issues of race heretofore rarely openly dealt with or discussed in Brazil's discursive racial practices. A Black graduate student and activist offered the following: "I thought I was listening to 10 militants from the Black movement dismiss racial discrimination but they were justices of the Supreme Court. . . . They echoed arguments that the Black movement had been making for two decades" (de Souza 2013). In particular, Barbosa, known for his sharp legal mind, expressed views that echoed the central premise of racialized social inequality and its historical reproduction in Brazil. He noted that for so long those who had benefitted from discriminatory practices had remained silent on racial issues, and only after racial minorities were given a perceived advantage did issues of race became more visible—but then only from the frame of their privilege. In other words, Barbosa implied that only until a disadvantaged social group is given a modicum of opportunity does discrimination become a political issue in the eyes of the privileged. Indeed, for the most part the largely white ruling elite in Brazil had remained silent during most of the twentieth century while Blacks and indigenous peoples were subjected to unequal and unjust treatment and racialized permanently as second-class citizens. The next chapter will place these debates in the context of Salvador and illustrate how Afro–civil society dealt with higher education and affirmative action.

6

Black Education, Affirmative Action, and Citizenship in Salvador da Bahia

The Steve Biko Cultural Institute and the Pré-vestibular
para Negros e Carentes Movement

This chapter builds on chapter 5 by amplifying and framing key debates pertaining to affirmative action in Brazil by focusing on the roles played by the Pré-vestibular para Negros e Carentes (PVNC), or Prevestibular for Blacks and the Poor movement, and by the Steve Biko Cultural Institute, founded in Salvador in the early 1990s. It situates Salvador and the Steve Biko Cultural Institute within the broader context of the PVNC movement. There is a noticeable gap in the affirmative action literature written on Brazil, as it usually privileges debates and strategies that unfolded in Rio de Janeiro (Telles 2004; Htun 2004; Bailey 2009; Lima 2012; Cicalo 2012). One noticeable exception is the work of Gladys Mitchell-Walthour, who focuses on Salvador and São Paulo: she examines how affirmative action policies were implemented and analyzes the political opinions of those who might benefit from such programs (Mitchell-Walthour 2012). Her research thus serves to expand the scope and depth of the debates and in doing so fills a major hole in the literature. Debates on affirmative action are crucial to understanding modern Brazil, and more in-depth studies are urgently needed. In particular it is necessary to expand the scope of the discourse to better understand how other regions in Brazil approached and tackled issues of affirmative action in higher education. The struggle over affirmative action (implementation and enactment) and the central role played by Black social movements in Salvador in making it a serious political issue are central to understanding the broader struggle for affirmative action and racial justice in Brazil.

This chapter therefore addresses a serious gap in the literature by examining the emergence and rise of affirmative action in Salvador; the role of Black formal politics in Salvador and affirmative action; the founding of the Steve Biko Cultural Institute and its role in sparking early affirmative action debates; and Afro–civil society and Black social movements as specific sites of Black knowledge, consciousness, and political mobilization. It traces the evolution of these interrelated phenomena by analyzing the rise of the free *pre-vestibular* courses and affirmative action debates from the 1980s to the present. It is argued that in the 1990s, the city of Salvador represented an important site of Black grassroots mobilization and heightened social consciousness: it is within this context that the Steve Biko Cultural Institute emerged as a concrete political project of the Black movement. It was during this time frame that Blacks in Salvador were seeking and winning political office (albeit in small numbers) at the municipal level. Equally important, the debates, discourses, and tactics unfolding in Salvador in the 1990s must be understood as integral to the larger "strategic puzzle," as they were central to understanding affirmative action initiatives across Brazil.

Focusing on the city of Salvador and the Steve Biko Cultural Institute offers extremely valuable insights into the following: broader discussions on the reproduction of racial inequality in education and the initial reaction of Salvador's ruling elite to affirmative action; the early pre-vestibular and Black student movement mobilization; early affirmative action initiatives; and how Afro–civil society in Salvador responded to and addressed these issues as they unfolded during the 1990s and early 2000s. The main idea is to critically examine and present a coherent picture of how the Steve Biko Cultural Institute emerged and the PVNC movement unfolded in the context of social mobilization in Salvador. The amplification of these debates serves to better frame the long-standing struggle of Afro-Brazilians for citizenship, human rights, and more specifically affirmative action in education. Moreover, it further underscores the crucial role of Black social movements and civil society in Salvador and their efforts to transform the idea of the free pre-vestibular courses and affirmative action in education into a concrete political project aimed at the Black masses. The previous chapter dealt with early emerging discourses regarding affirmative action in Brazil on the national and international level; now it is necessary to step back and understand a series of parallel processes that unfolded alongside these discussions as they pertain to racial and social equality in higher education in Brazil and Salvador. This chapter therefore adds a new layer and expands the lens in order to better comprehend affirmative action debates in Brazil while simultaneously underscoring the crucial role of Black social groups and Afro–civil society in Salvador.

The Genesis of the Movements for Pre-vestibular for Blacks and the Poor

Starting in the 1990s an ensemble of debates, interlocking strategies, and major initiatives regarding access to higher education and affirmative action were linked to larger discussions on the strategic options available for poor and Black students with respect to higher education in Brazil (Martins, Medeiros, and Nascimento 2004). Simply put, what mechanisms were available and needed for Blacks and poor students to increase their overall representation or at least have a fair shot at being admitted to university? As discussed in the previous chapter, all students seeking admission to university must take a vestibular, or college entrance exam, and most students in order to be competitive are encouraged to enroll in pre-vestibular courses to prepare for the main exam. These pre-vestibular courses as previously explained are extremely expensive and often Blacks and poor students simply do not have the money and requisite resources to pay for pre-exam courses.

The fact that many Blacks and poor students could not afford pre-vestibular courses served to structurally reinforce and cement their social exclusion from Brazil's very competitive higher education system.

It is against this canvas that beginning in the 1990s Blacks and other social movements created, organized, and implemented a series of free or low-cost alternatives to the traditional pre-vestibular exams. It is argued that the PVNC movement not only was central to chipping away at the discourse that claimed Brazil was a racial democracy but also played a significant role in deconstructing how racial and class differentials reproduced social inequality in Brazil's discriminatory higher educational system (González 2010). The system of higher education reproduced a dirty racial and class calculus as Blacks and the poor were largely denied access to higher educational opportunities while white, upper-, and upper-middle-class students thrived and were successful. The PVNC as a grassroots articulation therefore emerged as a legitimate response and direct challenge to the inherent structural inequality of the university entrance exam system while at the same time democratizing higher education.

The basis of the PNVC movement is in the work of Abdias Nascimento, who created one of the first free exam courses for Afro-Brazilians as early as the 1970s, organized and implemented by the Center for African Brazilian Studies (Martins, Medeiros, and Nascimento 2004). By the 1980s this model was being replicated by the workers' union of the Federal University of Rio de Janeiro (UFRJ), which created a model directly tailored for associates and relatives of UFRJ employees and individuals with low incomes. By 1991, the Mangueira Vestibular program had been organized by local community groups in the Rio favela of Mangueira (dos Santos 2010, 199). In 1992, other programs took off and were replicated in states like Bahia, where the Steve Biko Cultural Institute was founded. Biko, however, was unique as it catered specifically to Salvador's largely Black urban poor population, who had been historically excluded from university education in Bahia. The Biko initiative as well as other similar models had major repercussions within the Black movement (dos Santos 2010, 199). Other networks and models were launched, such as Educafro (Education and Citizenship for Afro-descendants and the Poor), located in Rio de Janeiro and other states, and the Movement of People without University (Movimento dos Sem Universidade), which operates in several states (dos Santos 2010, 200).

According to Renato dos Santos, an expert on affirmative action and pre-vestibular programs, the PNVC movement is the outcome of a number of strategies of the Brazilian Black power movement of the 1970s and 1980s, which articulated the education of Blacks as a conscious political project—first because it serves to construct and strengthen existing leadership and second as a strategy of spreading and disseminating antiracism into new spaces of struggle and intervention (dos Santos 2010, 200).

The PNVC ideas were born within the structural logic of an oppressive and rigid social system where Blacks were locked out and excluded from the educational systems, resulting in limited or no upward social mobility. According to the Brazilian Institute of Geography and Statistics (IBGE), the percentage of nonwhites with a university degree was roughly 2.2 percent in 1997, compared to 9.6 percent for whites. By 2007 there was a slight increase (13.4 percent for whites and 4 percent combined for pardos and prêtos), but the gap between whites and nonwhites actually increased (Brazilian Institute for Geography and Statistics 2008).

These dismal numbers reflect the huge disparity between whites and nonwhites and suggest that nonwhites are not achieving eligibility for more competitive positions. In order to effectively compete in the labor market Blacks must go to university, but in order to get admitted they need requisite skills and training to prepare them for the vestibular. Thus the logic of the free pre-vestibular attempts to address these underlying structural symptoms. Free and open pre-vestibular courses challenged the inherent elitism of Brazil's discriminatory higher education system while simultaneously repositioning debates by putting educational democracy on the agenda (dos Santos 2010, 200). It is against this backdrop that starting in the 1990s the free pre-vestibular movements for Blacks and poor people spread like wildfire across Brazil in the form of grassroots mobilization, and it became integral to emerging debates on education as a core organizing principle linked to democracy, human rights, and citizenship.

The Rise of Black Rights and Affirmative Action in Salvador da Bahia: The Founding of the Steve Biko Cooperative

Starting in the late 1980s in Salvador and across Brazil, education as a political and human rights issue emerges as a strategic part of the Black movement's social agenda. In Salvador pointed questions were being asked: Why are there so few Blacks attending the main federal university in the state of Bahia, the Federal University of Bahia? What are the main obstacles to getting admitted to the Federal University of Bahia? Why are there hardly any Black professors and no courses on Afro-Brazilian history? Why are there hardly any Blacks in law, medicine, and science? These knotty questions heretofore texturally submerged set the stage for a series of hot counter-discourses—that is, ideas that directly contradicted the notion of racial democracy—on the status and position of Blacks within the Bahian and the Brazilian educational systems. Moreover, Bahia as a Black state and Salvador a majority-Black city, as well as the exclusion of Black people from educational opportunities, only served to further underscore the apartheid-like social relations and magnify the second-class status of Blacks in this region of Brazil. The 1990s, however, ushered in a radical new correlation of forces as issues of racialization and racial inequality were linked and became legitimate topics of conversation and not necessarily taboo as before. Enter Steve Biko; the social atmosphere in Salvador had by then become ripe for deeper and more sustained discussions on a series of key structural questions, such as the nature of Black oppression; the racialized criminal justice system, known for its harsh treatment of Blacks; the near-exclusion of Blacks from the professional labor market; the lack of political representation; and, of course, the role of Blacks in Bahia's educational system.

The Steve Biko Institute, founded in one of the Blackest geostrategic areas of the African Diaspora, was born as a Black resistance organization to challenge and address racialized inequality in higher education: its signature stamp was then and still is offering pre-vestibular courses to Salvador's Black urban poor majority at little or no cost.

Simultaneously, a new racial calculus emerged in Salvador as the social terrain was being altered by a repertoire of radically different antiracist strategies and discourses. This period witnessed the following social processes: the formation of Black student groups like the National Seminar of Black Students (Calmon 2014), the continued consolidation of MNU and the institutionalization of the blocos, the emergence of the left-leaning Workers' Party (PT) as a force in local politics, the electoral campaigns of more Black candidates who were seeking and winning local office on the municipal level in small albeit significant numbers (Martins, Medeiros, and Nascimento 2004), and of course, the founding of the Steve Biko Institute. At the same time, the old historic district of Pelourinho was being revitalized and repositioned as part of the larger urban strategy to make Salvador a major player in Brazil's ever-expanding tourism and carnival industry. The intersection and institutionalization of these forces were directly linked to broader strategic debates and larger discourses unfolding across Brazil regarding questions of racial identity and more specifically the reproduction of racial inequality in Salvador; previously silent and below the radar, racial inequality emerged as a key political question and serious social issue. Black movement activists, Afro–civil society groups, and some Black politicians began to analyze and speak more openly about racism and the specific ways racial inequality is manifested as well as reproduced in higher education and other areas. It is argued that this period provides a critical snapshot and extremely useful frame to better understand the emergence of the Steve Biko Institute as well as affirmative action debates in Salvador and Brazil; it was in fact a rich historical and political moment in the social history of Salvador.

Steve Biko's trajectory must first be seen alongside the rise of the National Seminar of Black Students, which grew out of the National Union of Students. The National Seminar of Black Students was first organized in Salvador in the first half of 1992 after it was decided that there was a need for an organization tailored to the special needs of Black students (Cerqueira 2013). The National Union of Students during this time placed a priority on issues like the quality of education, better campus housing, and transportation. However, Black students in Salvador wanted to address a different set of issues: while they were in agreement with the basic demands of the National Union of

FIGURE 6.1. Yvete Sacramento was one of the first Black female deans in Brazil (Salvador). She was an early advocate of affirmative action and implemented some of the first programs of that kind in the 1980s and 1990s. She currently serves as minister of reparations for the mayor's office of Salvador, Bahia, and is the only Black person in his cabinet.

Students, many Black students wanted more flexible school schedules, longer library hours, and the amplification of courses focused on Black themes. Some students had jobs while others were forced to travel across Salvador, sometimes having to take two buses in order to reach the university on time for classes. At the same time, deeper and more structural issues surfaced about the lack of Black students and professors, the lack of courses on Black history, art, and philosophy, the hardships Blacks faced getting into the university, and of some of the serious problems associated with the vestibular.

One of the central issues was not only affirmative action per se but the strategies and mechanisms available to get more Blacks admitted to the university. By early 1992 a group of Black students came together to evaluate how they might address some of these issues; after a series of intense debates and long discussion, it was decided that the National Seminar of Black Students would form their own study group; it was first organized to help them study and share basic information so they could do better in their registered courses at the university. Later the idea was transformed, and they then decided to offer a special study program aimed at helping Black and low-income students prepare for the vestibular (Cerqueira 2013). Many had friends and family members preparing for the vestibular, therefore this idea emerged as a natural strategy. So in early 1992, a few months shy of Steve Biko's founding, the National Seminar of Black Students started offering free vestibular classes for Black and poor students at the Federal University of Bahia. These courses were already spreading like wildfire across Brazil and represented new ways of thinking about college admissions and university education.

The Rise of the PT, MNU, and Black Politics in Salvador

At the same time it is important to note that by the early 1990s the MNU chapter of Salvador had established its social identity as a leading Black movement group and its organizational roots were firmly in place. According to David Covin, Salvador's MNU chapter at this time was the most active, aggressive, capable, and inspired chapter in Brazil; it was the leading and most organized chapter given that it provided the core of the national leadership, published a journal, and had a core cadre of forty dedicated militants. Additionally, it had roughly two hundred active members at its disposal. It had also established its headquarters in the neighborhood of Liberdade (Covin 2006, 131). In 1992, MNU made a conscious decision to become more aggressively involved in local politics and implemented its Black Political Project, which called for supporting local candidates for municipal office. Simultaneously there was an early fusion of some MNU members with the PT, which was in the process of establishing itself as a serious political party in Salvador and across Brazil during this time period. MNU's racial discourses proved crucial to early debates on racial discrimination and social inequality as they emerged within the Workers' Party; MNU members were instrumental and played key roles in placing these debates on the table as well as shaping the Workers' Party's early discussions and strategies pertaining to Afro-Brazilians and racial questions. MNU and the evolving PT were crucial to how issues of racial discrimination were unfolding in Salvador.

As MNU was gaining traction in Salvador by entering local politics, the Workers' Party was making inroads and becoming a serious political party on the national and local level in Brazil. By early 1992, after years of party preparation, recruitment, and outreach, the Workers' Party was emerging as an important player in local Salvadoran politics. According to Rosa Fernandes, an early Workers' Party militant who rose through the ranks, the early 1990s were breakthrough years for the Workers' Party in Salvador. As a young leftist she joined the Workers' Party in the 1980s, and in 1992 she was elected to the post of secretary of participation, which oversaw recruitment, political education, and grassroots mobilization. It was during this time that the Workers' Party was becoming more involved in local politics and had to field candidates for mayor, city council, and other offices on the municipal level. Fernandes adds that starting in 1992, discussions of racism and racial discrimination arose as serious political issues (Fernandes 2013). The PT, according to Fernandes, had to address racial discrimination not only in Salvador but also within the ranks of the party.

Moreover, issues of affirmative action within the Workers' Party, the recruitment and promotion of Black candidates, and the larger role of Blacks in the Workers' Party surfaced as key subjects of debate (Fernandes 2013). The Workers' Party locally and nationally as a left-leaning party had a fairly strong critique of class inequality but did not have a deep understanding of racial issues, according to Fernandes. Again issues of race and their understanding of racial discrimination stood in the shadows of racial democracy. Fernandes observes that there was very little real discourse around race within the Workers' Party in Salvador, despite its majority-Black population; issues of race were in fact structurally absent within the left-leaning Workers' Party. Black party militants therefore had to wage an internal fight within the Workers' Party in order to push the party to think more strategically and structurally about racism and racial inequality. In addition to being pushed for by Fernandes, these initiatives were led by Katia Carodosa, Luiz Alberto, and Nilo Rosa, all MNU party members. "It was a double fight because along with the traditional aspects of party organizing, Black members had to wage an internal fight within the PT" (Fernandes 2013). The PT during this time in Salvador rarely articulated race-specific platforms, but individual candidates were able to do so.

At the same time, the Workers' Party also began to promote more Black candidates on the national and local level, as with Benedita da Silva's campaign to become to the first Black woman mayor of Rio de Janeiro and, in Salvador, the campaign of Luis Alberto for local city council. They were not successful but da Silva would later serve as governor of the state of Rio de Janeiro, and Alberto was later elected to serve as federal deputy. The opening of these new spaces coincided with a new phenomenon—the rise of Black political candidates in Brazil and Salvador seeking political office. As the Workers' Party struggled to address and articulate issues of racial discrimination, during this time more and more Black political candidates were running for local political office (this phenomenon will be addressed more specifically in the next chapter). In 1988, singer and songwriter Gilberto Gil from the Partido Movimento Democratico Brasileiro (Party of the Democratic Movement) was elected to Salvador's city council, making him one of the few elected Black officials in Salvador and Brazil in the late 1980s. In 1992, four more Blacks were elected to Salvador's city council. The 1990s saw the institutionalization of Black electoral politics as more and more Black candidates sought office in Brazil and Salvador.

According to Odiosvaldo Vigas, first elected to Salvador's city council in 1992, the local political elite had long been excluding Blacks from political power. He says that up until the early 1990s, Blacks were structurally absent from local and state politics in Bahia (Vigas 2013). It was his identification with the U.S. Black power movement and other Black movements across the Diaspora that first inspired him to seek political office in Salvador. He argues that despite Blacks being a numerical majority, Salvador's social structure had kept Blacks permanently locked out of power and at the bottom. Historically, Blacks were excluded from the carnival clubs and owned few businesses, and the tiny Black middle class was weak, fragile, and divided and had no social consciousness or analysis of racial discrimination and its long-term impact on Black people in Salvador. Vigas, going one step further, argues that the institutional exclusion of Blacks from educational opportunities largely explains why Blacks have been so poor, marginalized, and powerless in Salvador (Vigas 2013). From 1888, when slavery was abolished, until the middle of the 1990s, when issues of racial inequality became more clearly linked to education and other issues, the Brazilian government did not address racism nor provide special aid or any type of assistance or programs for Blacks in areas of employment, housing, or education. However, the early 1990s were seen as opening new spaces to critically think about race relations in Salvador, as there was a radical new opening created first by the blocos and later by Black student activists and the first generation of Black politicians being elected to office in Salvador and across Brazil. By the time Vigas came to power in 1992 there was a realization that education was essential to social mobility and that Black political power under the right conditions could address racial inequality.

The Steve Biko Cultural Institute, 1992 to Present

In 1992, the Steve Biko Cultural Institute (SBCI) emerged as a grassroots organization born to challenge inequality in education. It was first called the Educational Cooperative, but in 1994 it renamed itself the Steve Biko Cultural Institute after the renowned South African political activist Steve Biko, a leading member of South Africa's Black Consciousness Movement who died in detention in 1977. Steve Biko is hailed a martyr of the antiapartheid struggle and his name is now synonymous with transnational Black freedom struggles. According to Lázaro Passos, a member of the board of directors and former teacher from SBCI, "Steve Biko is a reference for us because of his student activism, and above all else, he saw education as a weapon against oppression" (Passos 2013). The name Steve Biko, while of course symbolic, is an attempt to link the struggle of Afro-Brazilians to the broader Pan-African freedom struggle and transnational diasporic discourses. The founding of the SBCI is recognized as a rich historical moment in Salvador's burgeoning Black consciousness movement and the struggle for Afro-rights across Brazil.

It is important to recap that back in the 1970s, as discussed in chapter 3, the blocos and other groups in Salvador were criticizing racial inequality, altering the metrics of carnival participation, repositioning and promoting a more positive Black identity, and mobilizing large swaths of Black youth across Salvador. Issues of access to education and racial discrimination for Salvador's urban poor were central to these discourses, and by the late 1980s some blocos had already established their own schools and after-school programs that provided free (or low-cost) education and support services to students. The blocos were crucial to the social trajectory of this rising new Black consciousness and on some level must be credited with paving the way for the Steve Biko Institute's educational initiatives. Within this time frame the SBCI represents the continuation and concrete articulation of Black social movement ideas from the early 1970s that posited that Blacks were historically excluded from educational opportunities because of the way public and higher education were structured across Brazil.

In the 1990s, the SBCI seized a unique space, as it was founded as a cutting-edge Afro–civil society educational organization to address deep educational inequalities as well as provide systematic preparation for low-income Black students from public schools to be successful in the highly competitive vestibular exam and the university. In addition to advancing affirmative action since 1992, Biko's core organizational mission has been to serve and promote the social and political advancement of the Afro-Brazilian population through educational training and political engagement with an emphasis on positive Black social consciousness and identity (Cerqueira 2013). Its pedagogy, teaching, and training programs are mainly designed for low-income students with poor academic skills, as many students arrive with low self-esteem and extremely negative self-images. According to Passos, "students arrive after eleven years of bad schooling, often their self-esteem at rock bottom. We reach out to human beings and that is what matters. We always leave our mark" (Passos 2013). Biko, in addition to working to raise their academic skills for the vestibular, also works on preparing Black students to understand their place and positive role in Brazilian society as active social citizens.

Above: FIGURE 6.2. Sílvio Humberto, founding member of the Steve Biko Institute. He currently serves on the Salvador, Bahia, city council, being one of the more recent members of the progressive wing of the Black movement to be elected to local government. July 2013. Photo by author.

Left: FIGURE 6.3. Educational material for Steve Biko's Anti-Racism and Human Rights Program for Young People, 2001–2009.

The SBCI was founded in July of 1992 by a group of Black working-class university students in a small room on the campus of the Federal University of Bahia, the state of Bahia's premier institution of higher learning. Many of Biko's founders were the first to go to college in their families (Cerqueira 2013). From its founding in 1992 through the present, SBIC is credited with, first, being one of the first groups in Salvador to call for affirmative action in higher education; second, establishing the idea that the vestibular exams and prep courses should be free or at a lower cost to Blacks and poor students; and third and equally important, successfully organizing and establishing a credible alternative model of education by articulating a dynamic strategy based on the social realities of Salvador's urban poor. Many of these ideas later became part of relevant policy debates on affirmative action as well as a platform for direct implementation (Cerqueira 2013). The idea of organizing an alternative educational cooperative may seem inconsequential and unimportant from a distance, but in the context of Salvador's long, sordid racial history, the Biko Cooperative was a revolutionary project given the dirty calculus of racial politics as reflected in the low position and status of Blacks across the city and state. For the most part Blacks were structurally absent from Salvador's key social and political institutions during this time. Moreover, before Biko, Black students and their parents simply had no real options as they were completely shut out of Bahia's education system regarding college admission and affirmative action. Thus SBCI's radical new program opened new avenues and charted fresh territory in access to higher education. The SBCI's first class consisted of roughly twenty to twenty-five students, and 70 percent of them were later successful in their vestibular exams and were accepted into a university, according to Maria Durvalina Cerqueira, one of the founding members (Cerqueira 2013).

By early 1993 Biko changed locations and moved its office first to the neighborhood of Brotas, located in the central part of Salvador, and later to Barra. Given the success of their first class as well as the deep issues they were about to confront, Biko was forced to articulate its long-term vision, as it had some serious challenges to face. It needed, first, to develop the core of its organizational structure and organize a set of guiding principles; second, to professionalize its program in order to develop credible admission standards; third, to hire and train teachers in pedagogy and methodology; and, finally, to design a curriculum that catered to students with poor academic skills and low self-esteem and consciousness who faced serious challenges with regard to education. Their basic organizational structure was and to this day is along the following lines: pedagogy, administration, finance, political education, and social action. Their second class of 1993 consisted of two groups of fifty students. Classes were held in the afternoon and students were offered classes in Portuguese, literature, chemistry (organic and inorganic), math, physics, biology, geography, and history; and all classes were free or offered for very little (Cerqueira 2013). The main prerequisite was that all students who sought admission had to be enrolled in a public school and finishing their last year. The main challenge according to Sílvio Humberto, a founding member and ex–executive director, was to develop specific pedagogies, techniques, and methods that addressed issues of poor Blacks (Humberto 2013).

Enter Paulo Freire, as his ideas figured prominently in Biko's pedagogical plan; leaning on the Brazilian educator, Biko teachers sought to apply many of Freire's ideas by critically rethinking the role of education for historically oppressed and excluded communities. Based on Freire and using an integrated theoretical approach, Biko's pedagogy and methodology underscored the following: articulating a unique and more positive Afro-Brazilian aesthetic; deconstructing Brazil's and Salvador's thorny racial past by explaining slavery and its negative impact on Black Brazil; linking "race" to poverty and poverty to racism and social exclusion; challenging the myth of racial democracy; denouncing racism within the context of international human rights law; and valuing Blackness and positioning Blacks as having made contributions to Brazilian history. This was, of course, no easy task, and as Katrina Souza, a former Biko student, added, "We grow up seeing only whites having success as professionals and we learn that Black people were brought as slaves and all they left was a legacy of samba and capoeira and nothing more" (Souza 2013). The Brazilian higher education system in the forms of books, arts, social sciences, and the media simply did not address the role of Blacks in Brazilian society (except as slaves, criminals, and soccer players), resulting in their structural erasure from social history; and despite Brazil's having such a large Afro-population, it was as if Blacks did not exist.

By 1994, SBCI began to professionalize its work and became an official nongovernmental organization. During this time it began to train and prepare its own teachers in the area of capacity building, pedagogy, and methodology, because until that point many of its founding members had served as teachers; it also articulated another radical idea: free vestibular courses for Black and low income students. Simultaneously, it began deeper discussions on the role of Black students and the lack of Black professors within the university system in Salvador and Bahia. These strategic debates and discussions intersected with broader discourses in Salvador on more concrete ways to denounce and address racism as well as how to include Black people as active agents in Salvador's mainly white-dominated and -controlled social structure. Emerging from these debates was the idea to organize their "Citizenship and Black Consciousness" course as a thematic seminar for students studying at the institute.

The "Citizenship and Black Consciousness" seminar addressed key Black issues like land rights, police violence, the harsh and punitive criminal justice system, the political economy of racism in the labor market, and other key themes long structurally submerged in Brazilian social relations. The idea was to critically examine the often camouflaged inner dynamics of how Brazilian society operated while cultivating a critical social consciousness advocated by Freire. Along with preparing students for the vestibular by focusing on science and the humanities, the idea of the "Citizenship and Black Consciousness" seminar was to dig deeper in order to uncover the inner workings of an exploitative society that had naturalized racial inequality and oppression under the banner of racial democracy. According to Sílvio Humberto, in 1888, with the demise of slavery, Brazilian society deracialized race relations by declaring itself free of racial discrimination and in doing so it took the issue of race "off the table for almost one hundred years" (Humberto 2013). In the words of Humberto, who is an economist by training, the SBCI and the Black movement "placed the issue of racial inequality back on the table in order to challenge the prevailing hegemonic notion of racial democracy." It is against this

FIGURE 6.4. Maria Durvalina Cerqueira, founding member of Steve Biko, teacher, and social justice activist. July 2013. Photo by author.

strategic backdrop that in the early to mid-1990s Biko began its works to socially reinsert Afro-Brazilians into Brazilian history.

Between 1995 and 2005 were watershed years for the organization, as SBCI concentrated on getting more of its students into the federal university and won a prestigious award for its human rights educational programs. During this time affirmative action debates were simmering, and by early 2001 programs were being implemented slowly across Brazil. The SBCI had had success in getting students accepted

FIGURE 6.5. "Municipal Black Women's Day." Advertisement from the office of the Salvador city government. July 25, no year available.

into private universities, but now it concentrated more of its work on getting more students into the Federal University of Bahia (UFBA), the low-cost and more prestigious university in the state of Bahia (Silva 2014). Unlike in the United States, private universities in Brazil are less rigorous and don't carry the academic weight of the federal universities. Many of SBCI's students were getting into private universities but the aim between 1995 and 2005 was to get more of their students accepted into the premier university of the state. Perhaps one of SBCI's most significant achievements was its being awarded the prestigious National Human Rights Award by the federal government in 1999 in recognition of its groundbreaking work in the areas of education, pedagogy, and human rights. By the very end of the 1990s and the beginning of the 2000s, debates on affirmative action on the national and regional level across Brazil were at a fever pitch, and the idea of affirmative action had finally arrived: its implementation as a serious political project by the state and civil society had taken root. By the very early 2000s, universities had begun to implement the first phase of their affirmative action programs.

By the end of the early 2000s, SBCI became more institutionalized, and its name became synonymous with Black education, affirmative action, and human rights (Chagas 2013). According to Jucy Silva, the current executive director, "it was during these years that Biko consolidated its organizational and social identity rooted in the struggles of Black people." Silva joined Biko as an English teacher in 1999, becoming the director of pedagogy in 2005 and later the executive director; she believes that Biko is one of the most significant, positive, and tangible achievements of Black social movements, because ideas were transformed into reality. She adds that since 1992 Biko has served Salvador's urban Black population for more than twenty years, and currently its mission is clearer, more defined, and better focused than ever before (Silva 2014). According to Silva, here are some of its signature achievements:

- SBCI is now recognized as a pioneering educational institute, and its pedagogical methods are now recognized across Brazil as cutting-edge.

- More than one thousand students have studied at Biko and have been accepted into universities.
- More than five thousand students have taken the Citizenship and Black Consciousness Seminar.
- SBCI has made a significant contribution to the education of Black youth and reducing their vulnerability to delinquency, crime, drugs, and alcohol.
- SBCI has trained and fostered the development of two generations of young leaders.
- SBCI has played a strategic role in laying the foundations for as well as articulating early affirmative action ideas long before they were accepted by mainstream discourse.
- SBCI provided institutional support to other Black social movements in Salvador.

Affirmative Action Arrives in Bahia in 2001

Biko's work within the large trajectory of Salvador's social movement of the 1990s up through the present broke new ground by linking pre-vestibular courses to education and affirmative action as well as to larger discussions on racial equality, citizenship, democracy, and social justice for Black and poor students in Bahia. At the same time, there were other centrifugal forces at play, such as the National Seminar of Black Students, the blocos, MNU, the PT, and the rise of Black candidates, as they were all central to pressuring the state and civil society to accept affirmative action in higher education as a fundamental human right. It was Biko, however, led by Black, grassroots, organic intellectuals who worked tirelessly to successfully implement an alternative educational program, who provided free pre-vestibular training courses to scores of students from the ranks of Salvador's urban poor. By the early 2000s, its long-term strategic vision of affirmative action was slowly taking root. At the beginning of 2001 the State University of Bahia followed by the Federal University of Bahia in 2002 announced their plans for affirmative action in education.

Biko and the PVNC movement were central to opening up this new space for affirmative action; however, they cannot be expected to make up the aggregate deficit of Black student enrollments in Brazil and Salvador: it is not their legal or social responsibility. It is only affirmative action programs mandated and enforced by federal laws and measures aimed at federal universities that will make up the difference; and given the low percentage of Black Brazilians with college degrees, it will take generations. In 2001, the State University of Bahia was the first university in Bahia, and one of the first in Brazil, to implement affirmative action in higher education, second only to the University of Rio de Janeiro. Many erroneously assume that in Bahia the first university to initiate affirmative action was the more prestigious Federal University of Bahia, but it was not: the State University of Bahia announced its affirmative action program plans in May of 2001 (Sacramento 2013). In addition to the 45 percent of its seats reserved for Black students from public schools, two seats were set aside for indigenous students as well as two seats for people from quilombo communities (historically Black slave communities with special legal status). The State University of Bahia was the true pioneer in affirmative action in Salvador and Bahia, and its vision of affirmative action dates back to the early work of Yvete Sacramento, who as early as the 1990s strongly advocated for a change in how the school's vestibular was administered. The State University of Bahia began as a technical school in the late 1980s to serve Bahia's largely rural population and by the 1990s it had become a full-fledged university (Sacramento 2013).

In 1998, Sacramento became dean and developed programs more geared toward working-class and poor students. She added that the university had to "create a university that corresponded to demographics of its students, many of whom were rural and poor" (Sacramento 2013). The traditional vestibular was, according to Sacramento, designed for students who went to private schools, so she changed the nature of the vestibular exams administered by the university. At the same time, she trained teachers at the university to prepare for a different type of student as well as opened more slots and spaces. As a consequence the university was able to accept more students (Sacramento 2013). Thus, she was able to change the nature of the vestibular, prepare teachers, and open up new spaces in a relatively short period of time, thus putting the State University of Bahia ahead of the curve regarding affirmative action in Brazil. Her pioneering work has gone largely unacknowledged in discussions about affirmative action in Salvador and Brazil. Sacramento argues that she was able to implement these bold changes because the State University of Bahia was off the radar screen and considered less prestigious than the Federal University of Bahia. According to Sacramento she also provided advice to President Cardoso back in the mid-1990s when he began to strategize around affirmative action. Thus, with these programs in place and a firm foundation laid, the State University of Bahia announced its affirmative action program in 2001 and by late 2002 it was ready to admit its first class that included students able to enter because of the program.

As the winds of social change were blowing across Brazil in the middle of the 1990s, the Federal University of Bahia (Bahia's premier university) began to prepare itself to address the deep complexities and knotty challenges of affirmative action. In the face of the contradiction of Salvador being a mostly Black city and the university being mainly white (including professors, students, and staff), the university had come to a cold realization that it had no real studies or statistical data on student enrollment elaborated along racial lines: it had no idea how many Black students applied, the acceptance, denial, or graduation rates, nor vestibular scores. While recording racial data was becoming more common in Brazil, it was not widely practiced by universities in Bahia. In 1998, according to Delcele Mascarenhas Queiroz (2004), an expert on affirmative action who wrote her dissertation on race and gender in higher education in Salvador, the social landscape was shifting at breakneck speed in favor of affirmative action and the university had to catch up. It was in 1998 when the Federal University of Bahia initiated its first study ever to collect statistical data on students on the basis of race. The categories included Black, prêto, pardo, Indian, and white (Queiroz 2014).

The study's conclusion was shocking but hardly surprising: first it revealed very low enrollment numbers for Blacks (prêto/pardos); second, it found that most pardos and prêtos were enrolled in less-prestigious programs in the humanities (Queiroz 2004). And the representation was even worse for Afro-Brazilians, as the percentage was practically zero in elite programs of law, medicine, science, technology, and engineering. These numbers are mirrored in and consistent with other studies like the Brazilian Institute of Geography and Statistics's studies of 1997 and 2007 (Brazilian Institute of Geography and Statistics 2008). Moreover, she adds, collecting the data on race "was all very new because the university simply did not have a preexisting model to follow and had no idea of how to classify students according to race. It was all very difficult" (Queiroz 2004). However, with the early data, the university was able to slowly begin to prepare for its affirmative action program, which came about roughly five years later. In July 2002, the Federal University of Bahia in Salvador announced that 40 percent of spots in undergraduate and graduate programs would be reserved for Afro-Brazilians. UFBA's affirmative action programs reserve slots for public secondary students who are Black, brown, or indigenous. Also, slots are allocated to white public secondary school graduates. And, space allowing, Black and brown students from private secondary school may participate. Salvador and Bahia had finally come full circle as their two primary universities finally had plans in place to implement affirmative action programs.

According to Queiroz, these policies led to a new calculus of social relations. She posits that these new policies and major initiatives challenged the prevailing racial hegemonies of Salvador's white elite about how racialized practices worked in higher education (previously kept off the table). She says that, first, the gathering of data and statistics by the Federal University of Bahia revealed the severely marginal status of the Black population as well as how they had been systematically excluded from education, thus no one could deny or discount racism as a key factor, as it was an empirical reality; second, when serious discussions arose on the legitimate rights of Black people to have a fair shot at higher education there was a swift and negative reaction in white elite public opinion (and this was the case in Rio in the late 1990s and early 2000); and third, in Salvador the white elite and ruling elements wanted to talk more about class inequality and were extremely uncomfortable talking openly about racial inequality in general and racism in education in particular. It was an extremely difficult conversation since racial inequality in Salvador was heretofore texturally submerged; but, however uncomfortable, these ideas percolated and served to open deeper a discussion on race as well as a platform to address racial inequality.

The research by Queiroz and her observations deserve further reflection: it is crucial to drill directly into the inner logic of race relations in modern Salvador. Such attitudes, and the prevailing hegemonic discourse of the white elite, underscore the ways in which Blacks, a numerical majority, have been so effectively excluded and dominated by Salvador's tiny white minority and their discriminatory social and political institutions. Affirmative action debates undressed and revealed the naked forms of exploitation and how a society built and premised on Black slave labor reproduced its racialized social practices in the public sphere; not only did affirmative action directly address equality and inequality, but it also exposed the open sores of past exploitation by uncovering the inner workings of a highly unequal society that had kept Blacks locked out of educational and other social opportunities. The supreme irony of this white racial arrogance is that when white students of the ruling elite were benefitting from a free university system—while they already had a clear strategic advantage—there was total silence; however, as Blacks slowly began to chip away at this total dominance and to question racialized educational inequality by linking racial discrimination to education and demonstrating how it was reproduced, then suddenly there were sharp outcries from the white elite on how Blacks might benefit "unfairly" from such programs. There was of course no discussion on how white students had benefitted.

To return to Humberto's comments on race, "the Black movement had to put racial inequality on the table for Salvador's ruling hierarchy" (Humberto 2013). It is against this hegemonic backdrop and strategic setting that issues of affirmative action, citizenship, and human rights unfolded in Salvador over the previous two decades. The SBCI along with other Black groups must be credited with making affirmative action and its implementation a political reality for the vast majority of Salvador's and Bahia's student population. Salvador, one of the most racially unequal places in the Americas, represents a unique set of circumstances; Afro–civil society and the Black social movements in Brazil therefore had a special social and moral obligation to unpack the history of social marginalization and Black oppression as well as to challenge racial inequality by constructing and implementing new social opportunities for Salvador's largely forgotten urban poor. In doing so they made significant contributions to modalities of Black consciousness, advancing education, citizenship, democracy, and human rights.

7

Black Electoral Politics in Salvador from the 1970s to the 2000s

Black politics in Latin America as a subfield of political science is underappreciated and grossly under-researched. Regrettably there are few studies of Black formal politics in Brazil and Afro–Latin America; however, political scientists over the last two decades have started to make important inroads and to focus more on this under-researched and overlooked field. Political scientists like Michael Hanchard (1994), Ollie Johnson (1998, 2000, 2008, 2013), Bernd Reiter (2009), Bernd Reiter and Gladys Mitchell (2010), Cloves Luiz Oliveira (1997, 2010, 2013), Kwame Dixon (2008), Kwame Dixon and John Burdick (2012), Gladys L. Mitchell-Walthour (2009, 2010), and others have made important contributions to exploring and understanding Black politics in the Americas: their work has focused on examining and analyzing the following: Black consciousness, social mobilization, and grassroots movements; the exclusion and lack of representation of Blacks in political systems; the slow rise of Black candidates in congressional and senate races; Black voting habits in Latin America; the voting preferences of Black citizens; and more broadly the intersection of race and politics. This subfield is in urgent need of more studies that focus on racialized social hierarchies and forms of racial inequality that exclude and deny Afro-groups opportunities in political systems. Chapter 7 addresses this void by addressing Black politics in the region by exploring and analyzing the rise of Black electoral power in Brazil and Salvador from the 1980s to the present.

Antiracism and the Return to Democracy in Brazil:
The Case of Salvador

Brazil returned to democratic rule in 1985 even though some constitutional guarantees were established as early as 1978 (Green 2010; Johnson 2013). This new political opening offered a radical new landscape that allowed social movements and civil society to reinsert themselves into the political system. Afro–civil society understood the unique historical moment and immediately recognized that these changes offered critical new social spaces to articulate new demands. Afro–civil society and women's groups were instrumental in getting antiracist and antisexist laws included into the new constitution of 1988. For example, Article 5 of the new constitution made racism a crime and subject to punishment, thus reforming the outdated Afonso Arinos law, which treated racism as a minor offense. With this new political space, Afro–civil society, while by no means monolithic, is represented by a broad cross-section, and the diverse expression of many different groups began to give rise to deeper and more layered discussions on racialization, racism, and gender issues. These conceptual categories were now analyzed more rigorously and linked to poverty, employment, housing, education, criminal justice issues, media representations, and a broad range of civil and human rights violations. Simultaneously Blacks were slowly entering the formal political arena and occupying prominent positions in the government, on one hand, and recognizing their "Blackness" and talking more and more about race and racial discrimination, on the other (Johnson 2013). In fact, as many entered the electoral arena they saw themselves as "Black politicians" and "not politicians who are Black," representing a sea change in the politics of Brazil at this time.

Salvador and Bahia therefore offer a unique case study in the rise of Black politics in Brazil given their large and diverse Black population. Bahia is a state and Salvador is the largest municipality within the province of Bahia and is the third-largest city in Brazil. Salvador plays an important role in national politics and is central to Brazil's national identity. Despite Salvador being a majority-Black city and Bahia a mostly Black state, Afro-Brazilians there have not been well represented in the local (and state) political power structure, and to date, they have never elected a Black mayor of Salvador nor a Black governor of Bahia. Some in Brazil (and others beyond) find the relative lack of Black politicians in Salvador and Bahia symptoms of deeper, historically inscribed patterns of racial and social exclusion. Along these lines this chapter offers a gaze into the world of Salvadoran local politics, as it focuses mainly on modern-day Black electoral politics from roughly the early 1980s to the present—when Black candidates started getting elected to national, state, and municipal office. While not exhaustive, this chapter offers a thumbnail sketch of local politics and some understanding of how formal politics has unfolded in Salvador and Brazil over the past three decades.

Within the tangled complexity of racial hierarchies and the politics of exclusion in Brazil, the city of Salvador and the state of Bahia illustrate the sharp contradictions stemming from the historical reproduction of white political privilege and the ways in which historical patterns of racialized social inequality have worked to exclude Blacks from formal political and economic power. The case of Black electoral politics in the city of Salvador (and the state of Bahia) is a case in point. The fact that Blacks in Salvador are close to 80 percent of the population but have not been able to gain a modicum of political power within the city (and the state of Bahia) is confounding to many observers. Given the city's status as the capital of Black cultural production (or the "Black Rome of the Americas") and the center of strong Black consciousness movements, and known for its politically active Black population—many wonder out loud why Blacks in Bahia have not been more successful in getting elected to office at the municipal and state level. In other words, given Bahia's and Salvador's rich Black cultural formations and Black numerical strength, why has this not translated directly into tangible Black political and economic capital? Thus far Blacks in Salvador and Bahia have not been able to translate their cultural power into effective political and economic power. Even at the municipal level of government Blacks in Salvador and Bahia have had tremendous difficulties getting elected (and appointed) to local and state office.

Despite being the "Black Rome of the Americas," Salvador has never elected a Black mayor, although a Black man was appointed to the position back in the 1970s. This distinction is important, as it provides a frame with which to better understand the trajectory of local politics over the past thirty-five years. The story of how a Black man has served as mayor but was not elected is analogous to many Brazilian soap operas, because it offers many intriguing twists and turns. It unfolds as follows: Back in 1978, Mario Edvaldo de Brito Pereira was appointed by the military dictatorship (ARENA) to serve as the mayor of Salvador from 1978 to 1979. Given the brief nature of his appointment and the politics of the dictatorship, he was only a figurehead for the ARENA party. He served for only roughly a year and was eventually replaced with a candidate with long-standing ties to the dictatorship.

The Case of Edvaldo de Brito Pereira and Gilberto Gil

The cases of Edvaldo de Brito and megastar Gilberto Gil, both of whom launched campaigns for municipal office in Salvador in the mid-1980s, vividly illustrate some of the thorny problems Blacks faced as they entered the electoral arena in Salvador during this time. Starting in the 1980s, along with the blocos, a core group of Black activists attempted to make an impact on the electoral arena in Salvador. Working in tandem, the blocos and Black movement activists in MNU wanted to challenge and confront Salvador's all-white local political and social elite, who had historically effectively excluded Blacks from local, state, and regional office. It is argued that the interlocking networks and complex layers of social power; the intricate rules of the political game; Blacks' lack of capital, education, and training; a weak if not nonexistent Black intelligentsia; and the multiple and overlapping social constructions of Black identity are some of the key factors that have severely constrained Black political opportunities and crippled the few Black candidates who were able to enter the electoral arena for the first time in the 1980s and 1990s.

In the context of Black Salvador it is therefore crucial to underscore that Black identity and politics traverse broad and diverse class, ideological, gender, religious, and regional spectrums—to name only a few. Blacks in Salvador are active in many different political parties, from the most conservative to the most progressive. In other words, Blacks in Salvador approach politics from varying political, class, gender, religious (Candomblé, Catholicism, and Protestantism) regional (rural and urban), and ideological angles. Therefore in order to understand electoral politics it is crucial to understand the following: first, the ways in which Afro-identity intersects and overlaps with these constructs (ideology, class, gender, and religion); second, how these various identity constructions play out in formal politics; and third, how such complex constructions complicate the formation of what is generally and loosely referred to as Black electoral politics and how such constructs may cause divisions within Black politics or within the Black movement. Against this backdrop the campaigns of some early candidates for office are highlighted in order to examine the rise of formal Black politics and tease out Black identity in modern Salvador.

The 1985 mayoral contest between Edvaldo de Brito, an Afro-Brazilian, and Mario Kertész, a Bahian with Jewish roots, neatly illustrates some of the knotty problems of racial politics in Salvador at this time (Conceição 2010). Remember Brito had briefly served as mayor of Salvador from 1978 to 1979, being appointed by the military. By 1985, with the transition to formal democracy, there was a new political opening in Brazil and Salvador. More and more Black candidates were seeking office across Brazil. By the middle of the 1980s, Brito had distanced himself from ARENA and decided to run as a centrist candidate on the Brazilian Labor Party (PTB) platform. At the start of Brito's promising campaign key sectors of the Black movement (groups such as Olodum and Ilê Aiyê and some from MNU) supported his candidacy, but his campaign ran into some serious problems and soon fizzled. Despite his being from Bahia, a lawyer, a former dean, and a relatively well-prepared candidate, Brito's campaign was not able to galvanize or capture the imagination or support from Salvador's largely Black population.

Brito as one of the first Black candidates to seek office in Salvador in the post-dictatorship era faced an uphill battle from the start: first, he never received the full support of his party due to internal squabbling, and consequently his campaign never gained the traction and support it needed to win; second, because he was unable to secure and maintain the support of his own party, the Brazilian Labor Party, this raised a red flag with some sectors of the Black movement; third, by not gaining the support of his own party, he lost the support and confidence of key allies within the Black movement, mainly Olodum, although Ilê Aiyê continued their support. Without the full party support of the PTB, it was extremely difficult for Brito to defeat his well-financed opponent, Mario Kertész, who at the time had the full support of Salvador's ruling oligarchy, including many of the leading newspapers and media outlets (Conceição 2010).

Although Brito had at first secured key support for his campaign from João Jorge Rodrigues, the leader of the popular bloco Olodum, Rodrigues later decided to withdraw his support of Brito for reasons that to this day are not very clear. Several other Black leaders soon followed suit and chose to support and campaign for Kertész. Additionally, some elements within the Black movement attacked Brito as being unprepared for leadership, for his past affiliation with ARENA, and for not being in line with their goals and ideas. The Brito campaign essentially collapsed. Moreover, it is also alleged that Kertész bought off some Black movement groups by promising second- and third-rate jobs in city government to those who supported his candidacy. Brito was soundly defeated by Mario Kertész, who received 54.6 percent of the vote, followed by Brito with almost 30 percent (Conceição 2010). Many believe the failure to elect Brito to be a cruel irony: first his party chose not to support him, and then key segments of the Black movement withdrew their support. The irony is that during this time in Salvador there was a blossoming Black cultural movement seeking ways to challenge Salvador's historically white political system as well as increase Black representation. But even with strong Black cultural politics emerging at this time in Salvador, the city was not able (or willing) to elect Brito as its first Black mayor. Nevertheless his candidacy was historic, as he would be one of the first Blacks to run for mayor of Salvador, and others would soon follow.

Brito, reflecting back on thirty-five years of Salvador's jagged historical landscape, believes that his appointment as mayor even by the

FIGURE 7.1. Edvaldo de Brito was appointed mayor of Salvador in the late 1970s and was the first Black person to hold the position. To this day no other Black person has been in the mayor's seat. Brito served as vice mayor from 2008 to 2012 and currently serves on the city council. July 2013. Photo by author.

military dictatorship was a shift in the calculus of political relations in Salvador. The contradiction he points to is that even though he was appointed by the military dictatorship to be the mayor of a Black city, his own electoral campaign was unable to garner the support of important Black groups and key blocos a few years later. A largely Black electorate and key elements of the Black movement chose in his view a candidate of Jewish identity over a Black candidate from Bahia. He has not forgotten this and strongly believes it was the ultimate of betrayals by the Black movement and implies that the military regime was more forward-thinking than the Black movement during this time. However, Luiz Cloves Oliveira, a political scientist who studies Salvador politics, argues that it was Brito's past relationship to ARENA (the political party of the military) that was problematic and his death knell (Oliveira 2013). Oliveira posits that in the post-dictatorial period many wanted to move past the military regime and those associated with it were inherently suspect (Oliveira 2013).

Brito, however, accurately points out that in the 1970s and mid-1980s there was only ARENA, which was the official government party, and the Brazilian Democratic Movement (MBD), which the military had manufactured as the official opposition. In other words there were no other parties to belong to. The calculus of the Black movements' decision to support or not support Brito must be seen through this lens. Moreover, while Brito is Black, he did not have a real or substantive relationship with the Black movement during this time; however, he did underscore his Black identity and his Bahian roots in the campaign. However, his past association with ARENA and the lack of support from his own party and the Black movement, on one hand, and a well-financed opposition who had the unwavering support of the local ruling oligarchy, on the other, doomed his candidacy and was simply too much to overcome.

Brito firmly believes that Blacks in Salvador at this time simply were not ready to elect a Black mayor due to low levels of consciousness and strong internalized anti-Black feelings. He points to the deep divisions within the Black movement, and the fact that many Blacks in Salvador simply "could not vote for a Black person" may partially explain his defeat. He recalls a Black woman domestic worker saying, "I can't vote for him, because he is Black like me and knows nothing." The irony of such a comment is that Brito, like that woman and so many Blacks in Salvador, came from a very poor family, and like that woman, he suffered many of the same daily indignities of social discrimination: he recalls having to escort his blind mother through the streets of Salvador in search of medical assistance, back in the early 1950s, and being called names (de Brito 2013). He eventually worked his way through law school, served as dean of a university, and has held several important positions in the government, but despite his record of public service, many Blacks in Salvador refused to support his candidacy for mayor in 1985.

Equally confounding are the razor-sharp contradictions informing the discourse around racialization and the mayoral campaign of 1985: the Black domestic worker stated that she could not vote for him

FIGURE 7.2. From the campaigns of Edvaldo de Brito and his son, who both ran for congress in 2012. June 2012. In possession of author.

because he was Black, while some in the Black movement said he was not Black enough. Brito was once referred to as a "Black man with a white soul." According to Brito, this was one of the most serious insults anyone has leveled against him. Along with these bizarre complexities is another social layer: it remains a strange if not a twisted racial irony that Salvador's only Black mayor was installed by the military dictatorship but rejected by the masses. Salvador to date has not elected a Black mayor: Brito ran for the Brazilian senate in 2010; however, he was not successful (de Brito 2013). He is currently a distinguished elder statesman and continues in politics as he now serves on Salvador's city council and was vice mayor from 2008 to 2012.

Another interesting political scenario is the case of megastar, writer, composer, singer, and activist Giberto Gil, who was jailed briefly by the military dictatorship and then exiled from Brazil but made his return back to the country in 1972. The reasons he was arrested and jailed are still not clear (Green 2010). Upon his return from exile, he began to work on various cultural projects, and by the 1980s had become more drawn to politics; with the restoration of democracy, he, like Brito, decided to run for mayor of Salvador. In 1988 he announced his intention to run and launched his campaign as candidate of the Partido Movimento Democratico Brasileiro (Party of the Democratic Movement); however, the local ruling political elite, through a series of backroom deals, strong-arm tactics, and intimidation, forced him to withdraw his candidacy. The reasons are still unclear why the Party of the Democratic Movement would not support his candidacy, but he renounced his bid for mayor and instead was "encouraged" to run for city council, where he successfully won a seat. And despite Gil's stature, him being from Salvador, and his mega-fame as a singer, he was not able to compete, challenge, or maneuver against the local Salvadoran political machine during this period. However, his candidacy for city council was successful and he was elected in 1988. With his election he became one of the first Blacks on Salvador's city council and one of the few Blacks in public office in Brazil in the late 1980s. So Gil, like Abdias do Nascimento and Benedita da Silva, became part of the first wave of Blacks elected to political office in Brazil in the post-dictatorship period. Both Gil and da Silva would go on to serve as ministers in Lula's first presidential administration.

These cases serve to neatly illustrate that Black candidates for political office in Salvador needed more than modalities of Black identity to compete effectively within the complexity of local politics. It is of course crucial to note that the military dictatorship placed severe restrictions on who could participate in formal politics from 1964 to the middle of the 1980s, keeping Blacks and so many other groups locked out of the structures of power and decision-making. By the middle of the 1980s, and with the return to democracy, many Black candidates simply did not have the training, contacts, or financing and were "new to the complex rules of the game," according to Oliveira. Additionally, Oliveira believes that the legacy of racial discrimination and the lack of education and business opportunities left millions of Brazilians illiterate or semiliterate and thus prohibited from voting until the 1988 constitution. These are some of the deeper institutional issues at play, and within this contextual frame it is extremely important to understand the "structural silence of racism" (Bacelar 1999) and how it operates within social structures across Salvador, which is characterized by severe income inequality along racial lines, intrinsic segregation policies that govern the region, and a ruling oligarchy that has historically been white.

The Hegemony of Racial Silence: Blacks Know Their Place in Salvador

In Salvador the open secret has always been the starkly unequal forms of treatment and relationships between Blacks and whites as manifest in social inequality expressed with the cordiality "as long as Blacks know their place." According to Jeferson Bacelar, a racialized behavior penetrates Salvador's social institutions, and racist behavior is internalized by the overwhelming Black majority and white minority. A pact of silence thus emerges where despite the low standing of Blacks in all social structures (employment, education, health, housing, and politics) and other unequal forms of treatment, the contradictions between Blacks and whites remain unaddressed. Racial discrimination is normative and, therefore, remains socially cleansed from public discourse (Bacelar 1999, 88).

Within these hegemonic structures there is another social layer: not only are Blacks openly discriminated against, but raising the racial question or talking about it is seen as an affront, impolitic, and simply beyond the normative parameters of prevailing hegemonies. Any person or group attempting to do so was called a troublemaker or accused of using a U.S. racial lens to understand Brazil. This process of refusing to address racism and racial inequality is referred to continuously in this book as the textural submersion of racialization. Therefore, in the middle of the 1980s, when Black candidates sought office, they did so within the prevailing hegemonies and among suggestions (by both Blacks and whites) that Black candidates were not prepared, did not have the requisite training, and thus were not worthy of high political office.

Scholars and activists who know Bahia have consistently commented on the curious position of Blacks in Salvador. While they are the clear majority, it is still difficult even today to find Blacks in positions of political and economic power such as in public office, in commerce and small business, or even as stock clerks or saleswomen/men in local malls (Dzidzienyo 1971; Mitchell 2003; Perry 2013). Blacks in Salvador historically and currently occupy a very low position in the political economy, and the base of the Black working and middle class is weak and deeply fragmented, and they do not necessarily view themselves individually or collectively through the prism of Blackness or Black identity. With the rise of Blacks seeking political office in Salvador in the 1980s, many Blacks were cognizant that they were "Black"; however, many were not necessarily conscious of the systemic reasons why they were so poor and marginalized. During this time the Black majority of Salvador did not necessarily see their low standing as a function of racialized social inequality, as these issues were structurally silent and deeply buried within Salvador's hegemonic social structures. Moreover, the lack of an organized Black working and middle class and the absence of attendant modes of Black social consciousness in the context of the structural silence around racial inequality served to reduce and constrain the options available within a competitive political and economic arena. Thus the comment by the domestic worker regarding Brito must be viewed within this context and along these lines.

The pact or "hegemony" of racial silence serves to delink Black social consciousness, and other modes of Blackness, from Black oppression and social identity, and most importantly it disallows the articulation of a strategy to challenge racial inequality, causing a disjuncture between racist social oppression and the causes and consequences of that oppression. Therefore historically the use of Black identity and specific forms of Blackness has not been useful in local politics in Salvador and Brazil. In other words, framing issues in racial terms was a nonstarter. Black candidates, regardless of issues of racialization, must come to the table with a broad repertoire of skills, financing, support, and, most of all, an agenda that is able to speak to an electorate that is unsophisticated, divided, and fragmented. Few Black candidates in Salvador have historically run on racial themes or racial justice or simply as Black candidates. Moreover Blacks across Salvador (and Brazil) belong to a broad array of different political parties ranging from very conservative religious parties to left-leaning socialist parties.

The late 1980s nevertheless represented an important historical marker in Salvador's local politics as Blacks were entering more and more municipal races. Between 1988 and 1992 Afro-Brazilians in Salvador increased their representation on Salvador's city council from roughly 11 percent to roughly 34 percent (Oliveira 2010). By the early 1990s more and more Blacks decided to enter into local politics; the case of Luiz Alberto (founding member of MNU and the Workers' Party in Salvador) illustrates many of the problems progressive, left-leaning candidates faced—then and now—in Salvador. Alberto ran for city council in 1992, receiving support from MNU's Black Political Project and blocos. As one of the most recognized figures from the Black movement and longtime member of the Workers' Party, Alberto launched his campaign for Salvador's city council with much promise and fairly deep support.

As a candidate from the Workers' Party he ran a historic campaign, and his platform was "rejecting racial violence" (Covin 2006). His campaign underscored the history of Blacks as exploited workers and focused on constructing a more positive role for Blacks in Salvadoran society. However, despite the social and cultural logic of his campaign, which fused class and race analysis and spoke directly to the objective conditions of Salvador's urban masses and had the visible support of the Workers' Party, Olodum, and MNU, Alberto was still not elected. He was not, like Brito, associated with the right but rather with the left-leaning Black consciousness movement. And what is even more interesting is that during this time, while the PT was still in its infancy as a party, it was fairly strong, but despite this he still lost; and while

Alberto was not successful there were four other Blacks elected to Salvador's city council in 1992. However, Luiz Alberto later ran for the national congress and was elected as federal deputy in the Câmara dos Diputados (the Brazil National Congress), where he currently serves.

The Structure of Local Government and Political Landscape

The current mayor of Salvador, Brazil's third-largest city, is Antonio Carlos Magalhães, but he is known as ACM Neto; he was elected in October of 2012 for a four-year term starting in January of 2013 at the ripe age of thirty-three. Neto is from the center-right liberal party known as the Democratas (Democratic) and he is a scion of a powerful and prominent political family from Bahia. His grandfather Antonio Carlos Magalhães was the mayor from 1967 to 1970 and governor from 1971 to 1975, from 1979 to 1983, and from 1991 to 1994. Neto chose as his running mate Célia Sacramento, a Black woman from the Partido Verde (Green Party), who currently serves as the vice mayor. As vice mayor Célia Sacramento is one of the highest-ranking Blacks in local government. Neto has twelve cabinet secretaries—eleven whites and one Black woman, Yvete Sacramento, who is head of the Secretaria Municipal da Reparacão (Municipal Secretariat for Reparations).

Over the past two election cycles, from 2008 to 2012 and from 2012 to 2016, Blacks have occupied the position of vice mayor of Salvador. Edvaldo de Brito Pereira, who ran for mayor in 1985 unsuccessfully, as previously discussed, served as the first Black appointed mayor in 1979 and served as vice mayor from 2008 until 2012. And now the post is currently held by Célia Sacramento, a lawyer and accountant by training. According to Sacramento, while Blacks have made gradual but important gains in local politics, the fact that the last two vice mayors have been Black suggests that Blacks may be within striking range and perhaps able to elect a Black mayor by the end of the decade (Sacramento 2014). The position of vice mayor as a part of Salvador's municipal governing structure is largely symbolic and ceremonial and comes with no real power. Sacramento, however, believes the symbolism is both tactical and strategic: she argues that given the low status of Blacks and the structural racism in Salvador, it is still important to have Black people and Black women representing the city of Salvador. The imagery, she opines, is both powerful and relational but not enactive. She argues this symbolic Black cultural power in Salvador interrupts how whites have traditionally seen Blacks in Salvador. According to Sacramento, "I am not the washerwoman or domestic. I am the Vice Mayor of Salvador who came from a working class family" (Sacramento 2014). In Salvador, these are important words. Moreover, she posits, her position and the message is important given how Blacks are constructed and how the political system has locked Blacks out of power. Sacramento believes her role as vice mayor reflects the slow, gradual changes occurring in local Black politics and that she is part of the transformation. Sacramento believes that it is time for the people of Salvador to elect a Black mayor and that Neto will be Salvador's last white mayor. According to Sacramento, there is now a line of qualified Black leaders as well as a more sophisticated Black electorate who will support and elect a Black mayor (Sacramento 2014).

Sacramento's views must be placed within the logic of the currents and crosscurrents on the ground in Salvador. Neto's selection of Sacramento in an act of bold racial calculus was spot on. First, it allowed him to cloak his candidacy as well as his mayoral image in the idea of racial democracy, and second, Sacramento served as the perfect mirage for the symbolic manipulation of race, gender, and Black cultural capital, as the decision fits perfectly within the logic of Salvador's racial democracy. She is a Black woman from Salvador who grew up poor, one of twelve children, who worked hard and became vice mayor of Salvador. This pro-hegemonic symbolism fits well in the Salvadoran ruling elites' discourse and of course works on many levels: first, Blacks (and Black women) are extremely proud of her; second, the local white male ruling oligarchy is able to continue to rule without having made any significant or strategic concessions to the poor Black majority; and at the same time, the ruling oligarchy can pride itself on its progressive racial paternalism; it is the logic of racial democracy at its best but in the context of Salvador's tangled racial politics. These forces are at play as Blacks attempt to break the historical grip of the ruling oligarchy even as they (the oligarchy) look to find new ways of maintaining power. Neto has therefore proven to be smart, skilled, and an extremely astute politician. His decision to select Célia Sacramento as his running mate was seen as a bold choice, as it helped to solidify on some level the Black vote (which is nevertheless not monolithic) and Black women's votes while simultaneously providing some superficial ideological, gender, and racial diversity to his campaign. On the national level, the Democrats are generally viewed as a right-leaning party so his choice of a Black woman from the Green Party with social movement credentials was seen as shrewd if not good politics.

Neto so far has received praise from diverse sectors of Salvador's political communities and has proven adept at navigating the Câmara Municipal de Salvador (the Salvador city council) as he now can count on roughly thirty-three of the forty-one members for their support. He has increased taxes and plans to use the revenue to modernize Salvador's urban areas by upgrading the infrastructure—improving roads and highways and building more parks, hospitals, and health services. Across the city there are a vast number of long-overdue infrastructural projects under way aimed at neighborhoods, roads, parks, bus terminals, and highways that had been in disrepair but are now being upgraded. He has received good marks for streamlined social services and is largely credited with making them very effective and efficient as well as addressing some of the long-standing urban transportation issues. But the issues of transportation will need more attention. Salvador with a burgeoning population of roughly three million inhabitants does not have a rail or urban train system, so navigating the city is a bit difficult as one is obliged to depend on unreliable buses or to drive, which leads to bottleneck traffic congestion, overcrowded roads, and thick plumes of smog and pollution. As the city's population has grown over the past twenty-five years, no improved or efficient mode of urban transportation has been implemented to meet these new pressures.

The centerpiece of Neto's urban plan is to modernize Salvador, and his renovation strategy is to build a new mega–shopping center, Novo Aero Club e Parque Altantîco, which will be located on the northern end of Salvador toward the airport and near the ocean. The new shopping center will include condominiums, theaters, restaurants, fancy shops, playgrounds, and open-air parks. Built with local, state, and private money, it is estimated to cost around R$300 million, or

US$150 million. The project is being led by La Guardia Enterprises out of Austin, Texas, and it is estimated that it will create three thousand new jobs (Sacramento 2014). This urban strategy is intended to update Salvador's crumbling urban infrastructure by revitalizing its image and to attract more national and international tourism. Such urban development plans are of course not new. Since the 1990s, when Neto's grandfather was mayor and later governor, Salvador spent millions on revitalization projects, such as the restoration of old historic buildings, roads, neighborhoods, and the airport. Across the city and state, "tourism" projects—that is, projects aimed at making the city more amenable to both Brazilians and foreigners—are central to the city's image and ability to attract visitors.

The idea of upgrading the infrastructure and making Salvador more amenable to tourism has been part of development strategies since the 1990s. According to Keisha-Khan Perry, the situation in Salvador is characterized by the global urban construction practices so common across Brazil as well as in cities such as New York and Paris. Such plans are premised on modern urban visions, which include aesthetic repositioning of "ugly, dirty and mistreated" sites into what is clean and pure (Perry 2013, 150). Such plans for urban revitalization are coded and have deeper underlying meanings, as they sometimes require the removal of poor urban communities. Moreover, as with any plans for development there are calls by poorer constituencies to spend more money on social services like schools, health care, parks, and urban transportation. Neto's urban plans thus far on some level reflect the logic of neoliberal governments—that is, they focus on efficiently delivering basic social services, improved infrastructures, and increased spending on projects aimed at increasing investment, which in the case of Salvador means promoting tourism.

The Secretaria Municipal da Reparacão

One the most interesting if not altogether overlooked units of the local government in Salvador is the mayor's Secretaria Municipal da Reparacão (Municipal Secretariat for Reparations), which is one of twelve official cabinet positions of the mayor's office. Given the political

connotation of the word some might find it interesting that Salvador—
one of the oldest and Blackest spaces in the Americas, where slavery
was legal for centuries—has such a high-ranking secretariat of reparations. The mayor's office and city council both have an office of reparations, but they operate independently of each other. The office of the
Secretariat of Reparations is the direct result of Black social movement
demands and was created roughly ten years ago by then-mayor Antonio Ibassahy (Lumumba 2013). Reparations generally speaking seek to
recognize and address the harms suffered by the victims of systematic human rights violations, according to the International Center for
Transnational Justice (International Center for Human Rights). However, in stark contrast to what the term reparations actually means this
is not what it denotes in the context of local Salvadoran politics. In this
scenario the Secretariat of Reparations does not provide any financial
compensation or any type of material assistance to any community or
individual claiming historical injustices, nor is it configured to investigate, hear, or adjudicate legal claims, nor does it issue any kind of legal
rulings pertaining to past or present social injustices. Therefore, the
secretariat's name, however powerful, is a misnomer.

The office, which is mainly symbolic, serves as a unique mechanism
to channel Black demands directly to the mayor. Groups like MNU,
Ilê Aiyê, Olodum, the Center for the Defense of Black Communities,
and the Black Youth Movement—and others—had long demanded
that local government create a special secretariat to deal with Black
issues. According to Valdo Lumumba, executive assistant to Yvete Sacramento, who works at the secretariat, the creation of the Secretaria
Municipal da Reparacão stems from demands of the Black movement
and is one of the concrete benefits of the World Conference against
Racism held in Durban, South Africa, in 2001 (Lumumba 2013). After
the conference, the Brazilian government (both national and local),
in response to pressure from Black social movements, sought ways to
address the history of social exclusion and racial discrimination.

The secretariat is currently headed by Yvete Sacramento, who
brings some impeccable and airtight credentials to this post. She was
one of the first woman and Black deans in Brazil. She was elected dean

at the State University of Bahia in 1998, and while serving as dean she was an early affirmative action pioneer, as she was one of the first to implement these programs for students at the state level in Bahia. She opened the State University of Bahia to more students as well as created new ways to administer the vestibular. Given her experience in education as dean, and with her innovative approach to affirmative action, she was also an early advisor to former president Cardoso's initiatives regarding affirmative action and played a key role in the preparation for the World Conference against Racism. While on some level innovative, the Secretariat of Reparation has a very small budget and no legislative or investigative powers, and it is not able to issue reports on issues pertaining to racial discrimination or social exclusion. It is composed of several important bodies, including the Local Council of Black Communities, the Special Racial Observatory, and a Black Youth Commission that has a special educational program to combat racial discrimination. These bodies may make recommendations to the secretary, and she is responsible for keeping the mayor updated on the needs and status of various Black constituencies across Salvador (Lumumba 2013).

However, the inability to issue reports or conduct investigation limits the overall scope of its works. Moreover, the commission's work is often obscure, and given its low budget, it is difficult to project its image. As a largely symbolic and powerless agency, its overall work is only tangential to the larger needs of Salvador's urban poor. Nevertheless the work of the commission is important as it gives the sitting mayor political cover and at least in theory the ability to understand, respond to, and prepare legislative initiatives aimed at addressing the concerns raised by Black constituencies. It remains to be seen how Neto will respond to the specific needs of Salvador's poor Black majority. In his inaugural address there was no mention of social inequality, racial discrimination, or social exclusion, nor did he speak about the work of the commission.

The Câmara Municipal de Salvador

Currently the Câmara Municipal de Salvador (Salvador city council) is composed of forty-one city council seats, and currently Blacks hold eleven seats. The period between 1988 and 1992 was important in the history of Salvador as more and more Blacks were elected to the Salvador city council. The city council is composed of a diverse set of individuals and political parties, from the right to the center to the far left. The majority of Blacks elected to Salvador's city council hail from working-class backgrounds compared to its white members, who usually come from middle- to upper-class backgrounds (Mitchell 2009). But Afro-Brazilians in general and Blacks in Salvador tend to be affiliated with the Workers' Party (Johnson 2006; Mitchell 2009) more than with any other party. Tia Eron, a Black woman with strong ties to the evangelical movement, received the most votes in the 2012 election and was easily reelected to her fourth term to Salvador's city council. First elected in 2000, Eron became one of the first Black women to win a city council seat in Salvador. Eron has deep support across Salvador, is a member of the right-leaning evangelical Partido Republicano Brasileiro, and is part of the Black Evangelical Movement. Eron articulates a strong Black rights discourse and gender consciousness; she fights for the rights of the poor, Blacks, and women and is involved in educational projects across the city.

She argues that she is "breaking the paradigm" of what it means to be Black in Salvador. "I don't wear a dashiki, nor do I wear dreadlocks, and I do not practice Candomblé, nor am I a lesbian, nor was I ever part of the Black movement," Eron says. She goes one step further and adds, "I am not a stereotypical Black from Salvador." She then framed her argument using Malcolm X and Martin Luther King Jr. as examples. She argues that they both connected their social identity to politics and religion, one as a southern Black preacher and the other as a Black Muslim. "So, why can't I use my religion?" (Eron 2013). Moreover, she argues that, like King, she is also a Protestant. Eron believes that religion in Salvador is mainly used to divide Black people, and one of her key projects is to connect with different faiths—Candomblé included.

FIGURE 7.3. Tia Eron was elected to the Salvador city council in 2000, becoming one of the first Black women to do so. She is part of the evangelical movement and in 2015 was elected to the National Congress of Brazil as a federal deputy (thus she is no longer part of the city council). July 2013. Photo by author.

It is important to ask several questions: First, what does Eron mean by "I am not a stereotypical Black from Salvador"? Second, how is her consciousness informed by said stereotype? Her ideas are rooted in the notion that Black "evangelicals" are somehow less Black than those who practice Candomblé or who wear dreadlocks. Eron's views spotlight and serve as an example of the ways Black identity in Salvador has been constructed, portrayed, and marketed in Salvador and across the Diaspora. Her positionality underscores the structural nature of Black identity and consciousness. The axis of her social identities revolves around the following: race (Blackness), gender (female), class (working-class, grew up poor), religion (Protestant/evangelical), and politics (right-leaning). She thus on some level openly contests and challenges (at least in her mind) what it means to be Black in Salvador while at the same time she is "labeling" and stereotyping other Blacks based on prevailing social constructions.

Additionally, Eron is waging another fight, and it is within her party; she believes it does not understand (or care about) issues of race, which in her views are central to addressing the problems of Blacks in Salvador and Brazil. According to the Partido Republicano Brasileiro, Black people don't exist—only people. She argues that the party needs a critique of race and gender and must develop a plan to address racial discrimination (Eron 2013). She is extremely popular across Salvador and many wonder out loud whether she will run for mayor; and if she does run, some believe that she could become the first Black elected mayor of Salvador. In 2015, Eron was elected to the National Congress of Brazil as a federal deputy and is no longer a member of the Salvador city council.

Burdick (1993, 1998a, 1998b) and Selka (2007) have written extensively on the positionality of Black Pentecostals and their uneasy relationship with, and the perception of them within, Black social movements in Brazil. First, they have drawn our attention to the growing popularity of Pentecostalism; second, they have argued that these movements and forms of consciousness must be taken more seriously by Afro-Brazilian social movement leaders, politicians, and researchers; and third, they have suggested that Black identity in Brazil is interwoven in complex ways with African identity in other parts of the Diaspora. And like other scholars they have underscored how Black Pentecostals in Brazil are constructed as less political, more conservative, politically unsophisticated despite evidence to the contrary (Cleary and Stewart-Gambino 1997; Selka 2007), and for the most part underrepresented in major Black consciousness organizations; in stark contrast practitioners of Candomblé are constructed as "closer to Africa" and therefore more conscious and theoretically more politically active.

But despite the problems with such constructions Burdick and Selka have pointed out that the growing Pentecostal movement should be a point of deep reflection for Black social movements in Brazil and Salvador. Given their social and political potential as allies in the overall fight to dismantle racism and promote Black rights, Burdick and Selka suggest that evangelicals be taken more seriously and not written off. Burdick posits that perhaps evangelicals' identity, while generally hostile to racial identity, might foster other forms of antiracism through its discourse of human equality. And Selka, writing about evangelicals

FIGURE 7.4. An ad from Salvador's Secretariat of Reparations reminding citizens to denounce racism and violence against women during carnival. 2012. In possession of author.

FIGURE 7.5. Closing session of the Salvador city council, June 2013. Photo by author.

in Salvador, suggests that initiatives such as the Movimento Evangélico Progessista (Progressive Evangelical Movement, or MEP) could offer possible points of articulation between evangelical Christianity and the Black movement. Moreover, their (evangelicals') emphasis on electoral politics and their grassroots mobilization capacity, if harnessed properly, could positively impact the broader struggle against racism and social justice in Salvador and Brazil (Selka 2007, 96). These multiple and competing social constructions of identity regarding the modalities of Black consciousness operate within several hegemonic spheres in Salvador: these hegemonies are reproduced via the media, marketing campaigns, carnival, the tourism-industrial complex, Black cultural producers (blocos), and the state.

In sharp contrast to Eron, on the other side of the political spectrum is Sílvio Humberto, who was also elected to Salvador's city council in 2012. His election (with the Partido Socialista [PS] / Socialist Party) was viewed as a historical event and important victory for Black progressives across the city of Salvador. Holding a PhD in economics, Humberto is one of the founding members of the Steve Biko Cultural Institute and was until recently its executive director. Given the difficulty that Black progressives have had getting elected to local government, Humberto's election was viewed as a milestone in Black radical electoral politics in Salvador, as he is one of the first from the Black progressive movement to be elected to Salvador's city council. Building a grassroots movement from below, he ran a campaign that underscored "Educacão, Igualdade e Respeito" (education, equality, and respect) as the basis of citizenship for all of Salvador's citizens. His campaign drew support from students, blocos, and labor and religious groups (African, Catholic, and Protestant), as it highlighted the status of the urban poor, violence against youth, a failed public educational system, and the lack of governmental transparency (Humberto 2014).

Humberto's mandate is to work with local government, teachers, and students to address the poor quality of education and police violence. Currently he serves on three permanent committees on the city council: he is the president of the Comissão de Educacão, Esporte, Cultura e Lazer (Commission on Education, Sports, and Culture) and the Comissão de Reparacão (Commission on Reparations), which is separate from the Secretariat for Reparations, and he also serves as a member of the Comissão de Finanças, Orçamento e Fiscalização (Finance and Planning Committee). One of his first tasks as president of the Commission on Education, Sports, and Culture was to conduct a survey and visit some of Salvador's public schools in order to better understand the needs of teachers and students. On a visit to one school, A Escola Municipal Parque São Cristovão, Humberto learned that the school had gone one month without any running water. In many other schools the infrastructure was compromised, there was no running water, and classrooms lacked teachers and basic materials. Humberto said he was shocked at the dilapidated state of some schools (Humberto 2014).

Humberto is also addressing one of the most disturbing issues faced by Black youth in Salvador: the harsh, punitive, overwhelming, and sometimes lethal police violence used disproportionately against Black youths, who are the main victims of state aggression in Salvador.

FIGURE 7.6. A poster from Salvador's Secretariat of Reparations' Racial Observatory Committee: "The Eyes of the World are here." No date available. In possession of author.

Unilateral police violence against Black youths on one hand and inter-gang and individual violence on the other are probably the most urgent issues facing the citizens of Salvador if not Brazil as a whole. Humberto, given his long history as a movement activist, has witnessed the day-to-day police brutality facing Salvador's youth. As Humberto asks, "How can one say there do not exist harsh measures as one sees the genocide of Black youth? We have to understand that our Black youth are being exterminated" (Humberto 2013).

Humberto, unlike most candidates from mainstream political

FIGURE 7.7. Informational bulletin from the office of Sílvio Humberto to his constituents featuring his campaign motto, "Education, Equality, and Respect." 2013. In possession of author.

parties, has chosen to shed light on police violence and social cleansing as urgent issues to be addressed by the mayor, the city council, and civil society. On some level his presence on the local city council brings a fresh and radical perspective rooted in the idea that police violence is a political issue as well as a human rights issue. His election and his new role on the city council created a radical new political space to address issues historically downplayed. Long denied a voice in local politics, Humberto is now able to put issues on the table that were heretofore taboo. He articulates a Black radical democratic vision long absent in local politics in Salvador. According to Humberto, Salvador, as a site of Black political power, culture, and identity, must challenge the hold the Salvador ruling elite have on political power. He wants to deconstruct political and economic hierarchies that have kept Black people out of power and at the very bottom of the social pyramid. In a recent interview Humberto asked, what type of city do the citizens of Salvador want? He says that they must want more than the efficient delivery of social services. He believes that—along with social services—issues of education, equality, police violence, free expression, practice of all religions, and peace and security are critical to address.

This snapshot serves to illustrate the ideological and social complexity, diversity, and density of local politics in this city of 2.5 million people. Despite the rise of blocos, the Black consciousness movements, strong Afro-referenced identities, the bold articulation of a new Black politics (cultural and formal), the new historic opportunities for Blacks in Brazil starting in the 1980s, and the fact that Salvador is an important site of transnational Diasporic Black identity, Blacks in Salvador and the state of Bahia have not been able to make significant gains at the municipal and state levels of Bahian politics despite their demographic and numerical strength. They are in fact still grossly underrepresented in local politics in Salvador and Bahia. Many Blacks in Bahia, to some extent, attribute the underrepresentation of Blacks in government to racism (Mitchell 2009), but this is a double-edged sword given that, as Gladys Mitchell points out in her survey research, Black candidates rarely focus on racism or racial inequality in their political campaigns. However, Sílvio Humberto's 2012 campaign for city council to some extent addressed racial discrimination even though his main platform focused on education.

Some are extremely pessimistic about the prospect of Blacks gaining a major foothold in Salvadoran politics and its economic structure, while some believe that Blacks are making slow, gradual, and important gains in the electoral arena. In short the cultural power of Blacks thus far has not led to a better socioeconomic situation for the urban masses of Salvador. The reasons for this are not altogether clear but some include the historical disenfranchisement and exclusion of Blacks from the political system until recently (1980s); the intricate structure of local party politics and the complexity of the hierarchies of power; the fact that "negros não votom em negros" (Blacks don't vote for Blacks); and the tight grip of the white Bahian business elite, which they continue to use to control, rule, and manipulate local and state politics. To date, Salvador has not elected a Black mayor, and few Black candidates have sought the office.

Conclusion

This book has chronicled the struggle for racial justice and human rights by Afro–civil society in Brazil and Salvador. It has identified and defined Afro–civil society and placed it at the center of social relations in Salvador and Brazil. The main premise has been that civil society forms the conceptual and theoretical underpinning to understanding social and cultural citizenship, grassroots mobilization, identity constructions, and democracy and human rights. Afro–civil society builds on these novel conceptualizations by linking issues of racialization, modalities of Black consciousness, the repertoire of various Black identities, Black politics, Black oppression, grassroots mobilization, and the Black struggle for human rights to the core ideas of civil society in the Americas. In doing so, Afro–civil society challenges the normative underpinnings of traditional civil society while at the same time making it more conceptually and theoretically relevant to Black peoples and their forms of organization and cultures. Afro–civil society therefore represents a unique and novel lens for theorizing Black struggles for racial and economic justice and human rights in Brazil and across the Americas.

The main argument is that Afro–civil society, however uneven, imperfect, and contradictory, is nevertheless central to understanding Black politics and the struggle for human rights in Salvador and Brazil. Along these lines this research has called attention to the ways in which Black cultures confront, challenge, and are coopted by dominant systems of oppression and hegemonic domination. Afro–cultural formations in Salvador and Brazil are used, on one hand, by Black activists as a means of social mobilizations, and, on the other, by the state and commercial interests to fashion Brazil as unique and exotic. And while Afro–cultural formations may serve as a basis for social mobilization and a platform for Black consciousness, and despite Brazil being a Black country, of all of Brazil's people, Afro-Brazilians continue to be the poorest, hungriest, least educated, and most likely to be homeless, under- and unemployed, and discriminated against with respect to the administration of justice. The cruel irony is that with the abolition of slavery Blacks left the plantations for the favelas, thus becoming theoretical citizens and noncitizens, inhabiting a schizophrenic social geography of belonging and not-belonging simultaneously. Against this backdrop, my research aimed to underscore how Blacks in Salvador and Brazil have challenged, undermined, and called into question racialized social inequality. The repositioning of racial discrimination was made all the more difficult given that until recently there were "no racial issues" in Brazil according to normative discourses.

As this has been a modest study, there are of course still other key questions to be explored. It will be important to pay close attention to the following: the impact of the new affirmative action laws in Salvador as well as Black access to the university in Salvador and Bahia; how Salvador's slowly rising new Black political class will negotiate power away from the old white ruling hierarchy and how this will play out; given the deep history of racial discrimination, how the new Black political class will address (if at all) racial and social inequality in health, education, employment, and the media (digital and social); what kind of new economic opportunities and structures, if any, will be available for the masses of Salvador, who currently due to historically inscribed forms of discrimination are locked out of key positions or located at the very bottom of the economic pyramid; and how Afro–civil society, cultural groups, and blocos will respond to the rise of a new Black political class.

References

Interviews with the Author

Altino de Souza, Walter, Jr. 2013. Poet, social movement activist, and expert on blocos afros. Salvador, Bahia, Brazil, July 1.

de Brito, Edvaldo Pereira. 2013. Former mayor and vice mayor of Salvador, current city council member. Salvador, Bahia, Brazil, July 1.

Calmon, Trícia. 2014. Student activist and founding member of the Seminar of Black Students. Salvador, Bahia, Brazil, January 31.

Cerqueira, Maria Durvalina. 2013. Founding member of the Steve Biko Cultural Institute. Salvador, Bahia, Brazil, July 9.

Chagas, Michel. 2013. Graduate of and volunteer at the Steve Biko Cultural Institute. Salvador, Bahia, Brazil, March 7.

Eron, Tia. 2013. One of the first Black women elected to Salvador's city council. Salvador, Bahia, Brazil, July 10.

Fernandes, Valdísio. 2013. Movement activist and founding member of the Workers' Party in Salvador. Salvador, Bahia, Brazil, July 1.

Humberto, Sílvio. 2013. Founding member of the Steve Biko Cultural Institute, current alderman in Salvador. Salvador, Bahia, Brazil, March 4 and July 9.

Humberto, Sílvio. 2014. January 23 and March 4.

de Jesus, Antonio. 2014. Director of Escola Odolum. Salvador, Bahia, Brazil, January.

de Jesus, Viviane. 2013. Movement activist. Salvador, Bahia, Brazil, March 6.

Lumumba, Valdo. 2013. Coordinator for the Secretariat of Reparations for the mayor's office. Salvador, Bahia, Brazil, July 10.

Oliveira, Cloves Luiz Pereira. 2013. Professor of political science at the Federal University of Bahia and expert on Brazilian and Afro-politics. Salvador, Bahia, Brazil, February 21.

Passos, Lázaro. 2013. Member of the Steve Biko Cultural Institute. Salvador, Bahia, Brazil, February 29.

Pereira, Sonia. 2013. Community activist from the Association of Residents and Friends of the Historic Center. Salvador, Bahia, Brazil, February 25.

Queiroz, Delcele Mascarenhas. 2014. University professor and expert on affirmative action in Bahia. Salvador, Bahia, Brazil, January 24.

Sacramento, Célia. 2014. Movement activist and vice mayor of Salvador, 2012–2016. Salvador, Bahia, Brazil, January 27.

Sacramento, Yvete. 2013. Secretary of Reparations for the Salvador mayor's office and former dean of the State University of Bahia. Salvador, Bahia, Brazil, July 10.

Santos, Sueloi. 2013. Member of MNU. Salvador, Bahia, Brazil, July 6.

Silva, Jucy. 2014. Executive director of the Steve Biko Cultural Institute. Salvador, Bahia, Brazil, January 28.

Souza, Katrina. 2013. Former student at the Steve Biko Cultural Institute. Salvador, Bahia, Brazil, January 28.

de Souza, Raquel. 2013. Teacher at and member of the Steve Biko Cultural Institute. Salvador, Bahia, Brazil, March 5.

Vigas, Odiosvaldo. 2013. One of the first Blacks elected to the Salvador city council and former coordinator of the Salvador city council Office of Reparations. Salvador, Bahia, Brazil, July 11.

Published Sources

Agier, Michel. 1995. "Racism, Culture and Black Identity in Brazil." *Bulletin of Latin American Research* 14 (2): 245–64.

Alberti, Verena, and Amilcar Araujo Pereira. 2007. *Histórias do movimento negro no Brasil: Depoimentos ao CPDOC.* Rio de Janeiro: Pallas; CPDOC-FGV.

Alberto, Paulina. 2009. "When Rio Was Black: Soul Music, National Culture, and the Politics of Racial Comparison in Brazil." *Hispanic American Review* 89 (1): 3–39.

———. 2011. *Terms of Inclusion: Black Intellectuals in Twentieth-Century Brazil.* Chapel Hill: University of North Carolina Press.

de Almeida, Adjoa Florencia Jones. 2003. "Unveiling the Mirror: Afro-Brazilian Identity and the Emergence of a Community School Movement." *Comparative Education Review* 47 (1): 41–63.

Altino de Souza, Walter, Jr. 2006. "O Ilê Aiyê e a relação com o estado: Interfaces e ambigüidades entre poder e cultura na Bahia." MA thesis, Universidade da Federal da Bahia.

Alvarez, Sonia, Ernesto Dagnino, and Arturo Escobar, eds. 1998. *Culture of Politics, Politics of Culture: Re-Visioning Latin American Social Movements.* Boulder, CO: Westview Press.

Andrews, George Reid. 1988. "Black Workers and White: São Paulo, Brazil, 1888–1928." *Hispanic American Review* 68 (3): 491–525.

———. 1996. "Brazilian Racial Democracy, 1900–90: An American Counterpoint." *Journal of Contemporary History* 31 (3): 483–507.

Bacelar, Jeferson. 1999. "Blacks in Salvador: Racial Paths." In *Black Brazil: Culture, Identity, and Social Mobilization*, ed. Larry Crook and Randal Johnson, 85–101. Los Angeles: UCLA Latin American Center Publications.

Bailey, Lee. 2009. *Legacies of Race: Identities, Attitudes, and Politics in Brazil*. Stanford, CA: Stanford University Press.

Beato, Luciana Bandeira. 2004. "Inequality and Human Rights of African Descendants in Brazil." *Journal of Black Studies* 34 (6): 766–86.

Bourne, Richard 2008. *Lula of Brazil: The Story So Far*. Berkeley: University of California Press.

Brito, Richard. 2012. "Joaquim Barbosa é eleito presidente do STF." *Política*, October 12.

Burdick, John. 1993. *Looking for God in Brazil: The Progressive Catholic Church in Urban Brazil's Religious Arena*. Berkeley: University of California Press.

———. 1998a. *Blessed Anastacia: Women, Race and Popular Christianity in Brazil*. New York: Routledge.

———. 1998b. "The Lost Constituency of Brazil's Black Movements." *Latin American Perspectives* 25 (1): 136–55.

———. 2013. *The Color of Sound: Race, Religion, and Music in Brazil*. New York: New York University Press.

Butler, Kim. 1998. "Ginga Baina: The Politics of Race, Class, Culture and Power in Bahia." In *Afro-Brazilian Culture and Politics: Bahia, 1790s to 1990s*, ed. Hendrik Kraay, 158–76. Armonk, NY: M. E. Sharpe.

———. 2000. *Freedoms Given, Freedoms Won: Afro-Brazilians in Post-Abolition São Paulo and Salvador*. New Brunswick, NJ: Rutgers University Press.

Caldwell, Lia. 2007. *Negras in Brazil: Re-envisioning Black Women, Citizenship and the Politics of Identity*. New Brunswick, NJ: Rutgers University Press.

Carvalho, Jose Jorge. 2001. "As propostas de costa para negros e o racismo acadêmico no Brasil." *Sociedade e Cultura* 4 (2): 13–30.

Cesar, Raquel Coelho Lenz. 2003. "Acesso a justiça para minorias raciais no Brasil: E a ação afirmativa o Melhor Caminho? Riscos e acertos no caso da UERJ." PhD diss., State University of Rio de Janeiro.

Cicalo, André. 2012. *Urban Encounters: Affirmative Action and Brazilian Black Identities*. New York: Palgrave McMillan.

Cleary, Edward L., and Hannah Stewart-Gambino. 1999. *Power, Politics, and Pentecostals in Latin America*. Boulder, CO: Westview Press.

Conçeicão, Fernando. 2010. "Power in Black Organizing in Brazil." In *Brazil's New Racial Politics*, ed. Bernd Reiter and Gladys L. Mitchell, 187–95. Boulder, CO: Lynne Rienner Press.

Conrad, Robert. 1972. *The Destruction of Brazilian Slavery, 1850 to 1888*. Berkeley: University of California Press.

Covin, David. 2006. *The Unified Black Movement: 1978 to 2002*. Jefferson, NC: McFarland and Company.

Curtin, Phillip. 1969. *The Atlantic Slave Trade: A Consensus*. Madison: University of Wisconsin Press.

Davis, Darien. 1995. "Afro-Brazilian Women, Civil Rights, and Political Participation." In *Slavery and Beyond: The African Impact on Latin America and the Caribbean*, ed. Darien Davis, 253–62. Wilmington, DE: Rowman and Littlefield.

———. 2007. *Beyond Slavery: The Multilayered Legacy of Africans in Latin America and the Caribbean*. Lanham, MD: Rowman and Littlefield.

Degler, Carl. 1972. *Neither Black nor White: Slavery and Race Relations in Brazil and the United States*. New York: Macmillan.

Dellacioppa, Kara Z., and Clare Weber, eds. 2012. *Cultural Politics and Resistance in the 21st Century: Community-Based Social Movements and Global Change in the Americas*. New York: Palgrave Macmillan.

Dixon, Kwame. 2008. "Afro-Colombian Transnational Social Movements." In *Latin American Social Movements in the Twenty-First Century: Resistance, Power, and Democracy*, ed. Richard Stahler-Sholk, Harry E. Vanden, and Glen David Kuecker, 181–95. Lanham, MD: Rowman and Littlefield.

Dixon, Kwame, and John Burdick, eds. 2012. *Comparative Perspectives on Afro-Latin America*. Gainesville: University Press of Florida.

Dunn, Christopher. 1992. "Afro-Bahia Carnival: A Stage for Protest." *Afro-Hispanic Review* 11 (1): 11–22.

Dzidzienyo, Anani. 1971. *The Position of Blacks in Brazilian Society*. London: Minority Rights Group.

Feinberg, Richard, Carlos Waisman, and Leon Zamosc, eds. 2006. *Civil Society and Democracy in Latin America*. New York: Palgrave Macmillan.

Finley, M. I. 1968. "Slavery." In *International Encyclopedia of Social Sciences*, Vol. 14, ed. David L. Sills and Robert King Merton, 307–14. New York: Macmillan.

Gilroy, Paul. 1993. *The Black Atlantic: Modernity and Double-Consciousness*. Cambridge, MA: Harvard University Press.

———. 2000. *Against Race: Imagining Political Color beyond the Color Line*. Cambridge, MA: Harvard University Press.

Goldstein, Donna. 2003. *Laughter Out of Place: Race, Class, Violence, and Sexuality in a Rio Shantytown*. Berkeley: University of California Press.

Gomes da Cunha, Olivia Maria. 1998. "Black Movements and the Politics of Identity in Brazil." In *Cultures of Politics and Politics of Culture: Re-Visioning Latin American Social Movements*, ed. E. Sonia Alvarez, Evelina Dagnino, and Arturo Escobar, 220–51. Boulder, CO: Westview Press.

González, Mónica Treviño. 2010. "Opportunities and Challenges for the Afro-

Brazilian Movement." In *Brazil's New Racial Politics*, ed. Bernd Rieter and Gladys L. Mitchell, 123–38. Boulder, CO: Lynn Rienner Press.

Goodman, Amy. 2013. "Mass Protests Sweep Brazil in Uproar over Public Services, Cuts, and High Costs of World Cup and Olympics." Democracy NOW!, June 19, 2013. http://www.democracynow.org/2013/6/19/mass_protests_sweep_brazil_in_uproar.

Gordon, Edmond T., and Mark Anderson. 1999. "The African Diaspora: Toward Ethnography of Diasporic Identification." *Journal of American Folklore* 112 (445): 282–96.

Green, Garth L., and Philip W. Scher. 2007. "Introduction: Trinidad Carnival in Global Context." In *Trinidad Carnival: The Cultural Politics of Transnational Carnival*, ed. Garth L. Green and Philip W. Scher, 1–24. Bloomington: Indiana University Press.

Green, James, N. 2010. *We Cannot Remain Silent: Opposition to the Brazilian Military Dictatorship in the United States*. Durham, NC: Duke University Press.

Hanchard, Michael. 1994. *Orpheus and Power: The Movimento Negro of Rio de Janeiro and São Paulo, Brazil, 1945–1988*. Princeton, NJ: Princeton University Press.

Harding, Rachel. 2000. *A Refuge in Thunder: Candomblé and Alternative Spaces of Blackness*. Bloomington: Indiana University Press.

Hardt, Michael, and Antonio Negri. 2001. *Empire*. Cambridge, MA: Harvard University Press.

Hasenbalg, Carlos Alfredo. 1984. *Race Relations in Modern Brazil*. Albuquerque: Latin American Institute, University of New Mexico.

Hernández, Tanya. 2013. *Racial Subordination in Latin America: The Role of the State, Customary Law, and the New Civil Rights Response*. Cambridge, UK: Cambridge University Press.

Htun, Mala. 2004. "From 'Racial Democracy' to Affirmative Action: Changing State Policy on Race in Brazil." *Latin American Research Review* 39 (1): 60–89.

Ickes, Scott. 2013. *African-Brazilian Culture and Regional Identity in Bahia, Brazil*. Gainesville: University Press of Florida.

The Institute of Brazilian Geography and Statistics. 2014. September 18.

Johnson, Ollie. 1998. "Racial Representation and Brazilian Politics: Black Members of the National Congress, 1983–1999." *Journal of Inter-American Studies and World Affairs* 40 (4): 97–118.

———. 2000. "Racial Representation and Brazilian Politics: Black Members of National Congress, 1983–1999." *Journal of Inter-American Studies and World Affairs* 40 (4): 97–118.

———. 2006. "Locating Blacks in Brazilian Politics: Afro-Brazilian Activism, New Political Parties, and Pro-Black Public Policies." *International Journal of Africana Studies* 12: 170–93.

———. 2008. "Afro-Brazilian Politics: White Supremacy, Black Struggle, and Affirmative Action." In *Democratic Brazil Revisited*, ed. Peter R. Goldstone and Timothy Power, 184–209. Pittsburgh: University of Pittsburgh Press.

———. 2013. "Race, Politics, and Afro-Latin Americans." In *Routledge Handbook of Latin American Politics*, ed. Peter Kingstone and Deborah Yashar, 302–18. New York: Routledge.

Klein, Herbert S. 1986. *African Slavery in Latin America and the Caribbean*. New York: Oxford University Press.

Kraay, Hendrik, ed. 1998. *Afro-Brazilian Culture and Politics: Bahia, 1790s to 1990s*. Armonk, NY: M. E. Sharpe.

Lima, Marcia. 2012. "Affirmative Action in Brazil: Challenges for Inclusion." *ReVista: Harvard Review of Latin America*, Fall. http://revista.drclas.harvard.edu/book/affirmative-action-brazil (page no longer available).

Love, Joseph L., and Werner Baer. 2009. *Brazil under Lula: Economy, Politics, and Security under the Worker-President*. New York: Palgrave-MacMillan.

Lovell, Peggy A. 2000. "Gender, Race and the Struggle for Social Justice in Brazil." *Latin American Perspectives* 27 (6): 85–102.

Martins, Sergio da Silva, Carlos Alberto Medeiros, and Elisa Larkin Nascimento. 2004. "Paving Paradise: The Road from 'Racial Democracy' to Affirmative Action in Brazil." *Journal of Black Studies* 34 (4): 787–816.

Mitchell, Gladys. 2009. "Afro-Brazilian Politicians and Campaign Strategies: A Preliminary Analysis." *Latin American Society and Politics* 51 (3): 111–42.

Mitchell, Michael J. 2003. "Changing Racial Attitudes in Brazil: Retrospective and Prospective Views." *National Political Science Review* 9: 31–51.

Mitchell-Walthour, Gladys. 2012. "Racism in a Racialized Democracy and Support for Affirmative Action." In *Afro-Descendants, Identity, and the Struggle for Development in the Americas*, ed. Bernd Reiter and Kimberly Eison, 207–30. East Lansing: Michigan State University Press.

Montero, Alfred P. 2005. *Brazilian Politics: Reforming a Democratic State in a Changing World*. Cambridge: Polity Press.

Nascimento, Elisa Larkin. 2007. *The Sorcery of Color: Identity, Race, and Gender in Brazil*. Philadelphia: Temple University Press.

Nishida, Meiko 2003. *Slavery and Identity: Ethnicity, Gender, and Race in Salvador, Brazil, 1808–1888*. Bloomington: Indiana University Press.

Oliveira, Cloves Luiz P. 1997. *A luta por um lugar: Gênero, raça e classe: Eleições municipais de Salvador, Bahia, en 1992*. Salvador, Bahia: Serie Toque A Cor da Bahia.

———. 2010. "The Political Shock of the Year: The Press and the Election of a Black Mayor in São Paulo." In *Brazil's New Racial Politics*, ed. Bernd Reiter and Gladys L. Mitchell, 65–85. Boulder, CO: Lynne Rienner Press.

Perry, Keisha-Khan. 2013. *Black Women against the Land Grab: The Fight for Racial Justice in Brazil*. Minneapolis: University of Minnesota Press.

Pinho, Patricia de Santana. 2008. "African American Roots Tourism in Brazil." *Latin American Perspectives* 35 (3) 70–86.

———. 2010. *Mama Africa: Reinventing Blackness in Bahia.* Durham, NC: Duke University Press.

Queiroz, Delcele Mascarenhas. 2004. *Universidade e desigualdade: Brancos e negros no ensino superior.* Brasilia, Brazil: Liber Livro.

Reis, João José. 1993. *Slave Rebellion in Brazil: The Muslim Uprising in 1835 in Bahia.* Trans. Arthur Brakel. Baltimore: Johns Hopkins University Press.

Reiter, Bernd. 2009. *Negotiating Democracy in Brazil: The Politics of Exclusion.* London, UK: First Forum Press.

Reiter, Bernd, and Kimberly Eison. 2012. *Afro-Descendants, Identity, and the Struggle for Development in the Americas.* East Lansing: Michigan State University Press.

Reiter, Bernd, and Gladys L. Mitchell. 2010. *Brazil's New Racial Politics.* Boulder, CO: Lynne Rienner Press.

Ribeiro, Matide. 1995. "Mulheres negras brasileiras. De Bertioga a Beijing." *Revista Feminista* 3 (2): 446–32.

Riséro, Antonio. 1981. *Carnaval Ijexá.* Salvador: Corrupio.

Rodrigues, João Jorge. 1999. "Olodum and the Black Struggle in Brazil." In *Black Brazil: Culture, Identity, and Social Mobilization,* ed. Larry Crook and Randall Johnson, 43–51. Los Angeles: UCLA Latin American Center Publications.

Rodrigues da Silva, Carlos Benedito. 2012. "State and Social Movements in Brazil." In *Black Social Movements in Latin America: From Monocultural Mestizaje to Multiculturalism,* ed. Jean Muteba Rahier, 185–200. New York: Palgrave Macmillan.

Romero, Simon. 2012. "Brazil Enacts Affirmative Action Law for Universities." *New York Times,* August 30.

———. 2013. "A Blunt Chief Justice Unafraid to Upset Brazil's Status Quo." *New York Times,* August 23.

Romo, Anadelia A. 2010. *Brazil's Living Museum: Race, Reform, and Tradition in Bahia.* Chapel Hill: University of North Carolina Press.

Sansone, Lívio. 1995. "Nem somente preto ou negro: O sistema de classifição racial no Brasil que muda." *Afro-Ásia* 18: 165–87.

dos Santos, Renato Emerson. 2010. "New Social Activism: University Entry Courses for Poor and Black Students." In *Brazil's New Racial Politics,* ed. Bernd Reiter and Gladys L. Mitchell, 197–225. Boulder, CO: Lynn Rienner Press.

Schwartz, Stuart B. 1986. *Sugar Plantations in the Formation of Brazilian Society, Bahia, 1550–1853.* New York: Cambridge University Press.

———. 1992. *Slaves, Peasants, and Rebels: Reconsidering Brazilian Slavery.* Urbana: University of Illinois Press.

Scott, Rebecca, Seymour Drescher, Hebe Maria Mattos de Castro, George Reid Andrews, and Robert M. Levine. 1988. *The Abolition of Slavery and the Aftermath of Emancipation in Brazil*. Durham, NC: Duke University Press.

Selka, Stephen. 2007. *Religion and the Politics of Ethnic Identity in Bahia, Brazil*. Gainesville: University Press of Florida.

Silvestrini, Blanca G. 1997. "'The World We Enter When Claiming Rights': Latinos and Their Quest for Culture." In *Latino Cultural Citizenship: Claiming Identity, Space, and Rights*, ed. William V. Flores and Rina Benmayor, 39–53. Boston: Beacon Press.

Stahler-Sholk, Richard, Harry Vanden, and Marc Becker. 2014. *Rethinking Social Movements in Latin America: Radical Action from Below*. New York: Rowman and Littlefield.

Stam, Robert. 1988. "Carnival Politics and Brazilian Culture." *Studies in Latin American Cultures* 7: 255–63.

Sterling, Cheryl. 2012. *African Roots, Brazilian Rights, Culture and National Identity in Brazil*. New York: Palgrave MacMillan.

A Tarde. 1992. "Residents Expelled from Pelourinho."

Teles dos Santos, Josélio. 1998. "A Mixed-Race Nation: Afro-Brazilians and Cultural Policy in Bahia, 1970–1990." In *Afro-Brazilian Culture and Politics: Bahia, 1790s to 1990s*, ed. Hendrik Kraay, 117–33. Armonk, NY: M. E. Sharpe.

Telles, Edward 2004. *Race in Another America: The Significance of Skin Color in Brazil*. Princeton, NJ: Princeton University Press.

Turner, Michael J. 1985. "Brown into Black: Changing Racial Attitudes of Afro-Brazilian Students." In *Race, Class, and Power in Brazil*, ed. Pierre Michael Fontaine, 73–94. Los Angeles: Center for Afro-American Studies, University of California.

United Nations Committee on the Elimination of Racial Discrimination. 2003. "International Convention on the Elimination of All Forms of Racial Discrimination." CERD/C/431/Add.8, October 16.

Index

Partido Democrático Trabalhistas. *See* Democratic Labor Party

Partido dos Trabalhadores (PT, Workers' Party): Black politics and, 108–11, 137, 144; elections and, 1, 73; members of, 20, 21, 69, 73–74

Partido Movimento Democratico Basileiro (Party of the Democratic Movement), 110, 134

Partido Republicano Brasileiro, 144, 146

Partido Verde (Green Party), 138, 140

Party of the Democratic Movement. *See* Partido Movimento Democratico Basileiro

Passos, Lázaro, 111–12

PDT. *See* Democratic Labor Party

Pedagogical Educational Project, 54

Pelourinho: eviction and expulsion from, 27, 57; history of, 48–49, 52, 54, 56–57, 106; as World Heritage Site, 16, 56

Pentecostalism, 146

Pereira, Amauri, 67

Perry, Keisha-Khan, 8, 17, 24–25, 141

Petrobras oil company, 54, 58

Pierson, Donald, 15

Pinho, Patricia: on Afro-Bahian cultural productions, 19, 60; on *blocos afros*, 51, 52, 62; on "milking mama Africa," 16, 60; works of, 8, 17

Police violence, 7, 18, 64–67, 149–50, 152

Political prisoners, release of, 41

Popular Movement for the Liberation of Angola (MPLA), 50

Portugal: independence from, 32; slavery and, 5, 9, 12, 29–31, 34

Poverty: high rates of, 18; racism and, 69, 115

Prêtos (dark-skinned Blacks), 31, 47, 52

Pre-vestibular courses, 101–5, 108, 119

Pré-vestibular para Negros e Carentes Movimento (PVNC, Pre-vestibular for Blacks and the Poor Movement), 10, 100–101, 119; genesis of, 102–4

Progressive Evangelical Movement. *See* Movimento Evangélico Progessista

Pro-Uni scholarship program, 79–80, 97

PT. *See* Partido dos Trabalhadores

PTB. *See* Brazilian Labor Party

Puxada Axé, 49

PVNC. *See* Pré-vestibular para Negros e Carentes Movimento

Queiroz, Delcele Mascarenhas, 121–23

Quilombos (maroon communities), 28, 59, 87, 92, 120

Race: class and, 60, 95, 96, 137; gender and, 2, 40, 66, 70–72, 121, 139, 146; meaning of, 3; race science, 36; relations, 65–66, 88–89, 111, 116, 123

Racial classification: struggles over, 23; system of, 30–32, 47, 121

Racial democracy, 35; challenging myth of, 115–16; challenging tenets of, 83, 86; claim of, 103; contradiction to, 105; ideas of, 70, 75, 81, 105; issue of, 24, 109; logic of, 139; trajectory of, 96

Racial discrimination: affirmative action and, 78–79, 82–89, 91, 96, 98, 123; approach to, 70; debates on, 6, 47; denial of, 66, 76, 78–79, 89; discussions about, 4, 10, 75, 146; history of, 19, 156; issues of, 109–10; legacy of, 135; protests against, 65

Racial formations: modern foundations of, 32; study of, 7–8

Racial inequality: addressing, 63, 80, 82, 89, 93, 136; challenges to, 56, 112, 124, 136; discussion of, 78, 101, 122–23; issues of, 106, 111, 116; reproduction of, 106; studies on, 11, 125; subject of, 51

Racialization: in African Diaspora, 8; history of, 22; textural submersion of, 4, 78, 93, 105, 122–23, 136

Racialized Black body, 42

Racialized social inequality, 76, 98, 127, 136, 156

KWAME DIXON is associate professor of African American studies at Howard University. He is coeditor of *Comparative Perspectives on Afro-Latin America*.

CPSIA information can be obtained
at www.ICGtesting.com
Printed in the USA
JSHW040349180522
25996JS00003B/133